Preserve Them, O Lord

A guide for Orthodox couples in developing marital unity

by Father John Mack

CONCILIAR PRESS

Ben Lomond, California

ISBN 1-888212-01-2

Conciliar Press
P.O. Box 76, Ben Lomond, California 95005-0076

In Memory of:

The Archpriest Alexander Schmemann
my first instructor in the meaning
of the Christian mystery

and

The Hieromonk Seraphim (Rose)
my first instructor in the necessity
of Christian martyrdom

Table of Contents

A WORD BEFORE YOU BEGIN

FOR THOSE WHO ARE ENGAGED OR PLANNING TO BECOME ENGAGED:

Congratulations! The two of you have been led over time to believe that God desires you to marry. This is an exciting time. So many preparations—the dress, the reception, the guest list . . . In the hustle and bustle of getting ready for the "big day," it is important that you also spend time getting ready for the days which follow the "big day."

That's what this manual is about. In it you will find eight discussions of important aspects of marriage. Included in the discussion chapters are plenty of worksheets for you to fill out. These worksheets will help you apply the material presented to your own relationship.

HOW TO USE THIS MANUAL
You will notice in reading through this manual that I often recommend discussing a certain subject with your priest. I have prepared this manual as a framework for a series of premarital counseling sessions between an engaged couple and their parish priest or other counselor. If you

"He who finds a wife finds a good thing, and obtains favor from the Lord."
—Proverbs 18:22

> "When men and women marry, the union should be made with the consent of the bishop, so that the marriage be according to the Lord and not merely out of lust. Let all be done to the glory of God."
> —St. Ignatius of Antioch

have not done so already, I recommend beginning a premarital counseling relationship as soon as possible. A trained priest or counselor can help you detect problem areas you may not notice on your own, as well as help you work through solutions to these problem areas.

If you use this manual as part of a premarital program, please read each chapter and fill out the sheets *before* you meet with your priest or counselor. Come ready to discuss the issues raised honestly and openly. If you are not able to meet with a priest or counselor for premarital counseling, each of you should read the chapters and answer the questions separately, then come together to discuss your answers.

At the end of the book is a section containing supplemental readings and discussion questions. All of the supplemental readings are drawn from AGAIN Magazine articles. Conciliar Press has often received requests from priests involved in premarital counseling for reprints of these AGAIN articles, and we have now put these materials together in anthology form so that they can be more effectively used in this way. As you read through the eight main chapters, you will find gray boxes in the margins indicating that supplemental reading on a particular subject is available. Read through these supplemental reading sections and use the readings as a springboard for further discussion.

A WORD ABOUT PLANNING WEDDING DETAILS

It is important that you talk through all of the details of your wedding with your priest so that all things will be done in accordance with the canons and guidelines of the Church. I strongly recommend reading Supplement A, *Guidelines Governing Orthodox Marriages,* to acquaint yourselves with all of these guidelines.

Be prepared to talk about these things with your priest *before* you make specific plans regarding the date of the wedding, sponsors (bridesmaids, best man), etc.

AN EXHORTATION REGARDING DATING AND SEX

Let me be very blunt. Don't allow the physical aspect of your relationship to develop beyond what is appropriate before you are married, and please, don't allow the physical aspect of your relationship to become the most important! I know you love each other, and I know how close you feel when you touch each other, and hug and kiss . . . And I know you want to feel even closer and to experience more unity, but I warn you a few wrong steps here can be disastrous later on.

Failing to show restraint in the sexual area during courtship will keep you from developing the other areas of your relationship. Like a body-builder who becomes physically distorted because he has concentrated on only one part of his body, your relationship will be distorted by undue emphasis in one area. Sexual energy released outside of marriage is obsessive and controlling. Within marriage it is balanced by the sacrament itself and is a fulfilling part of a larger whole. Outside of marriage, lacking the sanctifying influence of the sacrament, it controls and ultimately destroys. Don't take a short-cut. It only leads to ruin.

IT'S TIME TO GET TO WORK

If you work hard at developing your relationship now, it will save you much grief later. Remember: an ounce of prevention is worth a pound of cure. So, roll up your sleeves and get to work. You won't regret it!

FOR FURTHER READING (for engaged couples):
Guidelines Governing Orthodox Marriages (Supplement A)
Sex and the Spirit of Our Age by Fr. John Weldon Hardenbrook (Supplement B)

FOR THOSE WHO ARE ALREADY MARRIED:

When I originally developed this manual, I had in mind couples who were planning to get married. My goal was to help them understand themselves, as individuals and as a couple, in light of the Church's teaching on marriage. As I have thought and prayed about the use of this manual, it has become clear to me that my original scope was too limited. For in a very real sense, the material presented in this manual is applicable not only to those who are planning to get married, but also for those who are already married. Whether you have been married for a year, ten years, or fifty years, you can benefit from working through this manual as a couple. Let me suggest to you a couple of reasons why.

First, many married couples never received adequate premarital counseling. As a result, many of the important issues raised in this manual have never been thought through or discussed between them. My experience as a pastoral counselor has shown me over and over again that ongoing marital problems are usually a result of this failure to talk through important fundamental issues. Married couples who submit themselves to the discipline of working through this manual will discover many opportunities to discuss important issues, and will find their understanding of each other and their marriage greatly enhanced.

Second, many married couples never take the time to rethink fundamental issues as they and their marriage mature. Life is not static, and neither are relationships. As we age, we change and we mature. The way we think, the way we respond, the way we love, the way we disagree—all of these change. The people who fell in love and were married five, ten, twenty years ago are not the same people today. They are different and their relationship is different. Marriage counselors often attribute marital breakdown and breakup to a failure in recognizing change has occurred. Don't get me wrong. It is not the change that is dangerous; it is our inability to recognize and grow together through this change which presents the difficulty. As a marriage matures, there is a need to readdress and rediscuss basic fundamental issues. Spouses need to recognize and accept the changes in each other, and learn to understand each other in transition. This manual, therefore, should not be used only once and then set aside. Rather, it is designed to grow with your marriage and provide a resource to which you can return again and again to reacquaint yourselves with each other and with your ever growing and changing relationship.

Third, many married couples were married with non-Orthodox attitudes and assumptions about marriage. As is the case with just about every issue of faith and practice, the Orthodox perspective is somewhat similiar to Western Christian ideas and yet, at the same time, vastly different. Just as converts to Orthodoxy have to learn to rethink their theology, so they need to learn to rethink their understanding of marriage. This manual is specifically designed to present an Orthodox perspective on marriage. It purposely tries to stick to the basics, to those issues which are fundamental and on which there is clear consensus in the Tradition. It obviously does not address every possible issue, nor does it attempt to take a stand on every question. Many questions are best left to the spiritual direction of the local priest under whose oversight the couple functions. What is presented in this manual, however, are important fundamental Orthodox presuppositions concerning marriage. Couples who convert should take the time to work through each chapter carefully, trying to analyze how their own relationship will be affected by the fullness of the Orthodox Faith.

HOW TO USE THIS MANUAL

You should have no problem using this manual as it is written. The vast majority of the questions are equally applicable to married couples and to engaged couples. Some of them will need to be answered in the past tense (i.e., change "Why do you want to get married?" to "Why did you want to get married?") but all of them can be easily adapted to your current situation.

Read the chapter and answer the questions individually first. Then, find a time to come together to discuss your answers. Let me strongly suggest that you schedule a time when the two of you can discuss these issues uninterrupted. Before you even begin the book, block out eight "date" nights when the two of you can be together for quiet discussion and reflection. Also, please don't separate the nights by more than two weeks! The chapters all build on each other. To get the best use out of the manual, you should go through the chapters consecutively in a concentrated time period.

At the end of the book is a section containing supplemental readings and discussion questions. All of the supplemental readings are drawn from AGAIN Magazine articles. Conciliar Press has often received requests from priests involved in marital counseling for reprints of these AGAIN articles, and we have now put these materials together in anthology form so that they can be more effectively used in this way. As you read through the eight main chapters, you will find gray boxes in the margins indicating that supplemental reading on a particular subject is available. Read through these supplemental reading sections and use the readings as a springboard for further discussion.

Let me also stress that if you have serious communication difficulties in your marriage, you should talk to your priest about meeting with him or someone he recommends to discuss the chapters. The goal of this manual is not more conflict, but enhanced marital unity.

To achieve this purpose you must firmly place this goal in the front of your mind at all times! Satan is very active and will do all that he can to pervert the process and promote division and disunity in your marriage. Let me assure you: his efforts will increase as your efforts towards unity increase. The questions you will answer and the discussions that will flow out of your answers will touch many relational nerves. Unlike an engaged couple's, your relationship has a history. And since it is the history of two sinful human beings, it is a history plagued with mistakes, failures, and sin. Furthermore, both of you will have different recollections of your common history. This is inevitable. Our remembrances of the past are filtered by our own personalities and our own personal histories. Satan will try to use your mistakes and your different perspectives to separate you from each other.

ARM YOURSELVES WITH HUMILITY, REPENTANCE, AND FORGIVENESS

Knowing Satan's tactics beforehand, you can arm yourself against him. Most importantly, you can prepare yourself for spiritual battle by embracing humility. A story from the life of Saint Macarius illustrates this point beautifully: "When Abba Macarius was returning from the marsh to his cell one day carrying some palm-leaves, he met the devil on the road with a scythe. The latter struck at him as much as he pleased, but in vain, and he said to him, 'What is your power, Macarius, that makes me powerless against you? All that you do, I do, too; you fast, so do I; you keep vigil, and I do not sleep at all; in one thing only do you beat me.' Abba Macarius asked what that was. He said, 'Your humility. Because of that I can do nothing against you' " (Ward, *The Sayings of the Desert Fathers*, pp. 129-30).

What is humility? Consider the following saying of Saint Macarius: "When I was small with other children, I used to eat bilberries and they used to go and steal the little figs. As they were running away, they dropped one of the figs, and I picked it up and ate it. Every time I remember this, I sit down and weep" (ibid., p. 136). How easy it would have been for Saint Macarius to have blamed the other boys and excused himself. After all, he didn't steal the fig. He was just sitting there, minding his own business, when it rolled in front of him. But his humility did not allow such reasoning. He sinned, he was responsible, and he would repent. So too, in your marriage, you must accept personal responsibility for your own failings. Looking back is hard. In our marriage relationships we all have sinned! Let's face it, we've blown it, and, in blowing it, we have hurt our spouse and our marriage deeply. Our pride tells us to make excuses, to blame our upbringing, our surroundings, or our spouse for our sin. To be humble is to accept the reality of your own failures. To be humble is to repent, to admit your own sins and failures without casting blame on others.

Consider another story. "They said of Abba Macarius the Great that he became, as it is written, a god upon earth, because, just as God protects the world, so Abba Macarius would cover the faults which he saw, as though he did not see them; and those which he heard, as though he did not hear them" (ibid., p. 134). How easy it is for us to judge others. In our marriages we are so good at seeing the faults of our spouse and pointing them out. As you go through this manual this temptation will increase. As you and your spouse discuss various things you will see abundant opportunities to correct your spouse, to set him/her straight, to tell him/her that he/she is wrong and how. Humility will require of you silence—even if you are right and your spouse is wrong! The goal of these exercises is not to find out who is right and who is wrong. The goal is marital unity. Marital unity will only come in the presence of humility. And to be humble is to refuse to judge the other; it is to cover the faults which we see as though we do not see them.

Saint Macarius the Great also said: "If we keep remembering the wrongs which men have done to us, we destroy the power of the remembrance of God. But if we remind ourselves of the evil deeds of the demons, we shall be invulnerable" (ibid., p. 136). In your marriage you may have been deeply hurt and/or disappointed by your spouse. As you and your spouse look back over your marital life, don't allow Satan to tempt you into replaying those hurts in your mind. Whatever your spouse has done to you or hasn't done for you, whatever his mistake, forgive! As Saint Macarius says, blame the evil on its source: Satan and his wicked demons. Hate Satan, despise him in your heart, and look with pity on the one who was deceived and trapped by him. Remember, you too have been deceived and trapped by Satan. Forgive your spouse that you might be forgiven by God!

THE IMPORTANCE OF CONFESSION

In conclusion, as you go through this manual together, let me encourage you to make ample use of the sacrament of confession. Sin's hold over us is broken when we confess our sins. Most of the problems in your marriage can be traced back to this spiritual source—unconfessed sin. Your marriage is a sacrament, and thus is more than a physical or legal reality. It is spiritual and operates according to spiritual principles. The Fathers say that confession is a second baptism, releasing the fullness of the grace of that

"Lord, receive me, a sinner, and hear my prayer of repentance. I acknowledge my sins and transgressions, voluntary and involuntary, known and unknown. I firmly resolve, with the help of Your grace, to turn away from my sins and to amend my life according to Your glorious name forever. Amen."
—A prayer of repentance

sacrament back into our lives. Let me humbly suggest that confession can also be thought of as a second marriage. When both husband and wife confess their sin to each other, and most importantly, when they confess their sins individually to God in the presence of His priest, the fullness of the grace of marriage is released afresh into their relationship.

Please don't try to renew or deepen your marriage by yourself! You will fail. Work together with the grace of God given you in Christ through His Church and you will succeed!

Notes and comments/ things to discuss:

1

AN ORTHODOX UNDERSTANDING OF MARRIAGE

What is marriage? Marriage is a sacrament which unites a man and a woman in Christ, so that "they are no longer two but one flesh" (Matthew 19:6). But what does this mean? What is the Orthodox perspective on marriage, and how can that help us expand our understanding of how two people can grow in love for and with each other? These are the questions I want to answer in this chapter.

For the Orthodox, the key New Testament passages concerning marriage are John 2:1-11 and Ephesians 5:20-33. Both of these are read during the wedding service itself, and both provide deep insights into the nature of marriage. In the first, Jesus Himself attends a wedding ceremony in Cana of Galilee. In being at this wedding, and in performing His first miracle there, Jesus forever blesses marriage and sets it apart as a "sanctified" way of life. In the second passage, after describing the various responsibilities of the husband and wife, Saint Paul makes the cryptic statement: "This is a great mystery, but I speak concerning Christ and the church" (v. 32). The word which is translated "mystery" is the Greek equivalent of the

> "From the beginning God has been revealed as the fashioner, by His providence, of this union of man and woman."
> —St. John Chrysostom

Latin word from which we get "sacrament." Thus, the Orthodox Church stands on solid biblical ground when it calls marriage a sacrament. But what does this mean? What does it mean for marriage to be a sacrament?

To understand the distinctive Christian understanding of marriage, it is helpful to review the two views of marriage which predominated during the time the New Testament was written.

The first view was that of the faithful Old Testament Jew. In his way of thinking, the goal and meaning of marriage was to be found in procreation. "Be fruitful and multiply," God commanded Adam and Eve. "I will bless you, and in multiplying you I will multiply your seed upon the earth," God promised Abram. To the faithful Jew the most obvious sign of God's blessing was the presence of children. "Behold, children are a heritage from the LORD, the fruit of the womb is a reward. . . . Happy is the man who has his quiver full of them" (Psalm 127:3-5). Undoubtedly, this emphasis on procreation as the sum of marriage was directly related to the dimness of the Old Testament's vision concerning the afterlife. Although the Jews were vaguely aware of a continued existence after death, prior to the advent of Christ, God had not revealed to the Jew anything about the nature of that existence. Therefore, the godly Jew looked to perpetuate his life through his offspring; hence, the central importance of childbearing.

The second common view was that of the Roman world, which is reflected in the legal statutes of the first century. Contrary to the Jewish understanding of marriage as a means to secure posterity, the Romans saw marriage as a legal contract entered into willingly and freely by two parties. The famous principle of the Roman law specified that "marriage is not in the intercourse, but in the consent." According to this view, the essence of marriage lies in the consent; it is a legal contract between two equal parties.

Although points of compatibility with both of these perspectives can be found in the Christian perspective, on the whole the New Testament finds them wholly inadequate to express the deep meaning of sanctified marriage.

MARRIAGE AS MYSTERY AND SACRAMENT

In the New Testament, because of Christ's work of redemption, marriage is raised to a new level of meaning which transcends human procreation and legal contracts. Marriage in the New Testament has become, in the words of Saint John Chrysostom, "the sacrament of love." Or, to use the expression of Father John Meyendorff, marriage is "a unique union of two beings in love, two beings who can transcend their own humanity and thus be united not only 'with each other' but also 'in Christ' " (*Marriage: An Orthodox Perspective,* p. 18).

This helps explain Saint Paul's reference to marriage as a "mystery." Throughout his epistles the term "mystery" refers to the new life which Christ came to bring to man. The "mystery" is the gospel, the pronouncement that man has been reconciled to God, and thus can live in and with God. When he, therefore, proclaims marriage to be a "mystery" of the Kingdom, he is proclaiming the awesome truth that the relationship of man and woman has been transformed (by the death and Resurrection of Christ) from something purely temporal into the realm of the eternal.

Father John Meyendorff explains: "By calling marriage a 'mystery,' Paul affirms that marriage also has a place in the eternal Kingdom. The husband becomes one single being, one single 'flesh' with his wife, just as the Son of God ceased to be only Himself, i.e., God, and became *also*

FOR FURTHER READING:

Marriage as Sacrament by Fr. John Meyendorff (Supplement C)
Marriage & Family as Sacrament by Fr. Gregory Wingenbach (Supplement D)

Page 17

man so that the community of His people may also become His Body. This is why, so often, the Gospel narratives compare the Kingdom of God with a wedding feast. . . . And this is also why a truly Christian marriage can only be unique, not in virtue of some abstract law or ethical precept, but precisely because it is a Mystery of the Kingdom of God introducing man into *eternal* joy and *eternal* love" (ibid., p. 22).

Now this may sound to you rather abstract and unconnected to your relationship, but I would suggest to you that the point being made is of crucial importance.

MARRIAGE IS ETERNAL

Even before I came to understand the Orthodox perspective on marriage, it always bothered me that when I attended weddings outside the Orthodox Tradition, in the wedding vows the statement was made, "until death do us part." It wasn't the morbid connotations which upset me; it was rather that something was being said about marriage which conflicted with my own basic desires. To say that marriage only exists "until death do us part" is to say that the relationship established between a man and a woman in marriage is limited to this world and to this life. It is to classify marriage as one of the things that "is passing away" (1 John 2:17). That concept of marriage just didn't ring true; it didn't satisfy my deepest longings.

For, as I looked within, what I wanted as a man looking to be married to a woman was a relationship which would transcend this world, a relationship which would endure and last beyond the limits of time; I was looking for a love which would know no end. The secular musician Jim Croce expressed my feelings well: "If I could put time in a bottle, the first thing that I'd like to do is save every day till eternity passes and then spend them with you. But there never seems to be enough time to do the things that you want to do once you find them. I've looked around enough to know that you're the one I want to go through time with."

Christianity as the consummation of man's deepest longings provides the fulfillment of this desire. The Christian gospel proclaims: Marriage is forever! The sacramental union of a man and a woman in Christian marriage is an eternal union; indeed, the "peculiarity of Christian marriage consists in transforming and transfiguring a natural human affection between a man and a woman into an eternal bond of love, which cannot be broken even by death" (*Marriage: An Orthodox Perspective,* p. 57). Father Alexander Elchaninov expresses the full import of these considerations with these pregnant words: "Marriage enables us to pass beyond the normal rules of human relationship and to enter a region of the miraculous, the superhuman" (*Diary of a Russian Priest,* p. 46).

THE GOAL OF MARRIAGE

Marriage is a pathway that leads both the man and the woman to union with God. As Saint John Chrysostom explains, "Use marriage chastely, and you shall be first in the Kingdom of heaven." How different this is from the goal most couples have as they approach the sacrament of marriage. Very often couples get married for the purpose of fulfilling certain needs which they have in their own personal lives. Therefore, they come to marriage expecting happiness, emotional well-being, personal satisfaction—without even having to work for them. When they don't get these things, they feel cheated or blame their spouse. Often these marriages end in divorce. As Orthodox Christians we approach marriage very differently. The goal of marriage is not the fulfillment of one's needs; rather, the goal of marriage is heaven!

What is the practical implication of this for

> "Marriage is more than human. It is a micro-kingdom, a miniature kingdom, which is the little house of the Lord."
> —St. Clement of Alexandria

married people? On the one hand, it brings a sense of relief and encouragement. Speaking personally, I love my wife dearly. My wife means more to me than anyone or anything in the world, and I'd rather spend time with her than do anything else. I would do just about anything to make her happy, and it deeply bothers me when I know that I have offended her. In my pre-Orthodox days as a Protestant Christian, I always felt guilty about this. Since I was taught I shouldn't love the things of this world more than God, I was plagued by the question, "Whom do you love more: God or your wife?"

What a relief it is for me to know that because marriage is a sacrament, I don't have to choose between God and my wife! My relationship with my wife is not a thing of this world, it is of the Kingdom! The road to God *is* the road I travel with my wife. I love God by loving my wife, and as I give myself completely to her in self-sacrificial love, I give myself to God. Because of the sacrament of marriage, I find God in communion with my wife—not by myself as a hermit.

Add to this the fact that finding God with my wife is something that I will do not only in this world, but throughout *eternity*, and then you have the makings of joy. How empty every other approach to marriage is in comparison.

MARRIAGE IS A CROSS

At the same time, the fact that heaven is the goal of marriage helps to explain its more difficult aspect. The way to heaven is the way of the Cross. This is the road Jesus travelled and it is the same road His followers must travel. The joy of eternal life is rooted in the pain of the Cross, and it is only as we embrace the Cross in Jesus' name that we will know the joy and power of the Resurrection. If we reject the Cross, we reject the joy of the Resurrection. Saint Paul, in Philippians 3, says that the power of His Resurrection cannot be known apart from the fellowship of His sufferings.

This linking of the Cross and the Resurrection is fundamentally important. Anyone who has been married knows that every marriage has its cross. No marriage is perfect and no honeymoon lasts forever. There is no "happily ever after" in this world. It takes work, and lots of it, to make a marriage succeed.

When my wife and I were married, her grandparents had been married sixty years. My wife's grandfather—an old, short Englishman—pulled me aside just after the ceremony and said, "Let me give you a hint. Do what she says in the beginning, because you will in the long run anyway, and it is easier if you just give up first." There is wisdom in this, isn't there? Not that a man should be henpecked. But to make marriage work, both partners have to cut off their self-will.

In my marriage, it is my will that gets in the way and causes all the problems. It is my stubborn, proud will that tells my wife, "My way is the right way, because it is my way. Do it my way." Pride and self-will are sin—sin that destroys my marriage, and sin that ruins my journey to heaven. For, sadly, I often insist on my own way not only with my wife, but also with God! This attitude will both keep me out of heaven and destroy my marriage. But if I repent and change my ways by taking up the cross of self-crucifixion and living a life of self-denial, my marriage will endure and, by His grace, an entry into the heavenly Kingdom will be opened to me.

Isn't this beautiful? This is what you as a married couple really need to understand. The Cross flowers. The cross—the cross that is in your marriage and that *is* your marriage—will flower with divine life if you embrace it and kiss it and carry it, and don't run off and try to get another cross.

"He who does not take his cross and follow after Me is not worthy of Me."
—Matthew 10:38

FOR FURTHER READING:

The Arena of Marriage
   by Fr. Marc Dunaway
   (Supplement E)

There is a wonderful monastic story about accepting the crosses we are given to bear. There once was a monk who hated the cross God had given to him, and was always complaining to God. Finally God took him into a room filled with all sorts of crosses and said, "If you don't like the cross I have given you, you may choose your own." The monk looked around and saw many huge crosses, other crosses with nails in them or blood on them. These crosses didn't appeal to him. Then he saw a beautiful little silver cross over in the corner, and he said, "I'll take that one." And God said, "That is the one you already have." God does not give us a cross we cannot bear.

In our modern culture, many people are lost in a world without eternal meaning—it is a nihilistic world. In that kind of world, it makes no sense to stay in a marriage when the thrill is gone and the suffering begins. It makes no sense if you don't believe in morality or eternity or love. When it starts getting rough, why stay?

But if working through the day-to-day difficulties of a marriage relationship becomes part of your labor to attain the Kingdom—because it requires a denial of self and an embracing of selfless love—then it becomes an event of cosmic significance, because it involves the overthrow of the satanic pseudo-kingdom and the planting of God's Kingdom here on earth. Then it has meaning, because then you are involved in something bigger than yourself.

This world is empty. It is passing away. Other faiths take a man of this world and make him a better man of this world. The Orthodox Faith takes a man of this world and makes him a man of the world which is to come. The same thing is true about marriage. The best marital counselor or counseling book available outside of the Orthodox Faith tries to take a marriage relationship and make it a great relationship of this world. Only

Orthodoxy takes a relationship and makes it a relationship of the world which is to come.

THE BLESSINGS OF THE WEDDING SERVICE

The prayers of the Orthodox wedding service superabound with references to this transformation effected by Christ's hand. Over and over the priest prays for God's blessing: "O most holy Master, accept the prayer of Your servants; and as You were present there, be present also here with Your invisible protection. Bless this marriage and grant to these Your servants a peaceful life, length of days, chastity, love for one another in the bond of peace, long-lived offspring, gratitude from their children, and a crown of glory that does not fade away. . . .

"Bless them, O Lord our God, as You blessed Abraham and Sarah. Bless them, O Lord our God, as You blessed Jacob and all the Patriarchs. Bless them, O Lord our God, as You blessed Joseph and Asenath. Bless them, O Lord our God, as You blessed Moses and Zipporah. Bless them, O Lord our God, as You blessed Joachim and Anna. Bless them, O Lord our God, as You blessed Zechariah and Elizabeth.

"Preserve them, O Lord our God, as You preserved Noah in the Ark. Preserve them, O Lord our God, as You preserved Jonah in the belly of the whale. Preserve them, O Lord our God, as You preserved the Three Holy Children from the fire, when You sent down upon them dew from heaven.

"Remember them, O Lord our God, as You remembered Enoch, Shem, and Elijah. Remember them, O Lord our God, as You remembered the Forty Holy Martyrs, sending down upon them crowns from heaven. . . .

"Give them the fruit of the womb, fair children, concord of soul and body. Exalt them like the cedars of Lebanon, like a luxuriant vine;

"Bless them, O Lord our God, as You blessed Abraham and Sarah. . . . Preserve them, O Lord our God, as You preserved Noah in the Ark. . . . Remember them, O Lord our God, as You remembered Enoch, Shem, and Elijah."
—a prayer from the Orthodox wedding liturgy

bestow on them a rich store of substance, so that having a sufficiency of all things for themselves, they may abound in every good work that is good and acceptable before You. Let them see their children's children as newly planted olive trees around their table; so that finding favor before You, they may shine like the stars in heaven, in You, our God."

Following these beautiful prayers—which answer all of our deepest desires as we enter into marriage and proclaim the fullness which God has made available to those who have entered freely into Christian marriage—the couple is crowned with beautiful crowns. Undoubtedly the symbolism of the crowning is so rich that no one explanation is sufficient. As many authors have pointed out, the crowns represent the way of martyrdom and remind the couple of their call to self-sacrifice and self-denial in marriage. But these beautiful crowns also represent the entrance of the couple, as a king and queen in Christ, into the joy of the Kingdom of heaven. The liturgy makes it clear: they are crowned by God Himself! At the wedding in Cana Jesus turned the water into wine; at each subsequent wedding Jesus transforms each human (earthly) relationship into a doorway to the eternal, a passageway to true life, an open door into true, unadulterated, deified humanity.

The psalm verses following the crowning ceremony proclaim this beautifully: "You have set upon their heads crowns of precious stones. They asked life of You, and You gave it to them; length of days forever and ever. You will make them most blessed forever; You will gladden them with the joy of Your presence." Having been crowned by God, the new couple is made one in and with Christ for ever and ever.

The final seal on this sacramental union is the sharing of the common cup. Originally this common cup was the eucharistic chalice; later it contained the presanctified gifts; now it is blessed wine. Even so, the connection of marriage to the Eucharist should not be missed, for the point being made is crucial. The life you two will share as a married couple is nothing other than the life of Christ! It is only as you partake of the flesh of Christ that you can be the flesh of each other. The life of your marriage, your shared joy, mutual love, and intimate eternal union, is possible only in Christ! This is wonderfully symbolized in the procession around the marriage table. The circle you make symbolizes your unbroken life together for eternity. The centrality of the cross and the Gospel placed on the table is a potent reminder that you can only remain together for eternity if you remain together united in Christ!

As Father Stanley Harakas summarizes: "For Eastern Orthodoxy, marriage is not simply an agreement of a man and a woman to share their lives together; nor is it a mere legal sanction. It is not performed by the couple themselves with the clergyman and the congregation as witnesses to their decision. Their union, based on their freely-willed decision to join their lives together as husband and wife, becomes sacramental because they are joined together as Orthodox Christians who are members of the Eucharistic Community sharing together the Body and Blood of Christ and receiving the grace of God for their union through the ministration of the whole Church in the person of Bishop or priest and in the presence of the gathered people of God" (*Guidelines for Marriage in the Orthodox Church,* p. 4).

THREE PRACTICAL APPLICATIONS

What we have been talking about in this chapter cannot be dismissed as "theology irrelevant to day-to-day married life." Every bit of practical advice I could possibly give you regarding how to make your marriage succeed is based upon this

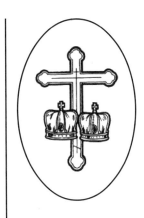

FOR FURTHER READING:

Now That You've Said "I Do"
by Fr. Peter Gillquist
(Supplement F)
Crown Them with Glory & Honor
By Fr. David Anderson
(Supplement G)

foundational theological framework. Let me end this chapter with three practical applications.

The Call to Preserve Your Marriage

First, the logical implication of this teaching is that divorce is contrary to God's will for your married life. Although it is true that the Church, on the basis of Christ's teaching, does allow for divorce, it is only tolerated because of human weakness (i.e. sin) and certainly it is never encouraged. God's mercy and grace is greater than our sin, and this includes the sin of divorce. "But from the beginning it was not so," reminds Jesus.

As you make a decision to be married in Christ, you are freely entering into a union which is eternal and which is full of God's life. To exit the marriage through divorce is wrong for you, not primarily because in so doing you will break a legal contract (the Roman view) and do damage to the generations which follow (the Jewish view), although both of these are serious issues. But the Church would insist that ultimately it is wrong, a bad choice, because to walk away from your marriage is to walk away from the love of God which is given to you in and through the sacrament. If a sacrament can be properly understood as a door into heaven, then the Church calls upon you not to shut the door—for in so doing you are shutting yourself off from God!

Divine Resources for Preserving Your Marriage

Second, the sacramental reality which I have discussed means that there are abundant resources available for you to overcome the inevitable difficulties which come with the married state. As you well know, relationships are not easy. We bring with us to our marriages an odd collection of hurts and habits which create friction and tension. We ourselves are too often proud, arrogant, selfish (the list goes on and on). Were it not for the sacramental reality of marriage, it would be hard to have hope for our marriages! As much as you love each other, you will have problems, and some of them will be major. In your own strength you are not and will not be able to overcome them all. The good news is that you don't have to try.

Father Anthony Coniaris helpfully explains: "Often we hear couples say, 'Nothing can be done to save our marriage. We can't start over again. We've made our mistakes and we're stuck with them. Now we have to make the best of it or quit.' As Orthodox Christians we do not subscribe to this thesis. We believe that there is something that can be done to improve marriage by God's grace. We believe that people can grow and change. Because of this, we believe that marriage has a potential for growth and change. No marriage is so good that it cannot be better, and no marriage is so bad that it cannot be improved—provided the persons involved are willing to grow together by God's grace toward the maturity of Christ who came 'not to be served but to serve' " (*Getting Ready for Marriage*, p. 14).

Preserving the Spiritual Perspective in Your Marriage

Third, the fact that a Christian marriage transcends earthly relationships and ushers the couple together into the Kingdom of God should remind you once again that the most important aspects of your relationship are not the material, but the spiritual. The fact that the marriage ceremony is a sacramental service of the Church should also remind you that you cannot know the full grace of God outside of living communion with Him in and through His Church, and especially through regular reception of the Eucharist. As Father John Meyendorff has noted: "Individual sacraments receive their true reality and their meaning only

> "Teach [your wife] the fear of God, and all good things will flow from this as from a fountain, and the house will be full of ten thousand blessings. If we seek the things that are incorruptible, these corruptible things will follow."
> —St. John Chrysostom

if they lead to or express the corporate life of the Church" (*Marriage: An Orthodox Perspective,* p. 61).

Since I have been blunt with you before, let me be blunt again. There is nothing the adversary would like better than for you to lose focus in the beginning years of your marriage. Most couples get married with material plans and goals. This is healthy and good and should be encouraged. Dream together! It's fun and it can bring you closer. But be careful! For very often, young marrieds can be so obsessed with meeting their material goals that the spiritual is put on hold, or even forgotten for a time. What they don't realize is that by forgetting the spiritual they are sowing seeds of marital disunity and unrest into the newly plowed bed of their marriage. Sadly, it is these seeds which later grow and strangle the love of many marriages. Be smart! "Seek first the kingdom of God and His righteousness, and all these things shall be added to you" (Matthew 6:33).

To help you think through the issues raised in this chapter, consider the following questions carefully. After you have answered them yourself, discuss your answers with your partner.

1. Before you read this chapter, what was your understanding of the nature and purpose of marriage?

_____

_____

_____

_____

_____

_____

_____

_____

2. How does this understanding differ from the Orthodox

understanding as explained in this chapter?

_____

_____

_____

3.   Walk through the wedding service point by point. Refer to the full text of the wedding liturgy from a service book, as well as the explanations given in this chapter and in supplemental readings F and G. Discuss together the meaning of each of the prayers and actions of the liturgy.

   a. What is being promised during the betrothal? What is the meaning of the exchange of rings?

_____

_____

_____

   b. What is the significance of the procession to the front of the church after the betrothal? Reflect on the words of Psalm 128.

_____

_____

_____

_____

   c. What do the wedding crowns signify?

_____

_____

_____

   d. When you hear the epistle reading, what is its message to you personally? What does the Gospel reading say to you?

_____

_____

_____

_____

_____

e. What is the significance of the cup of blessing? How is this different from the eucharistic cup?

_____

_____

f. What is the meaning of the circular procession or "dance of joy"?

_____

_____

4. Do you feel you are willing and able to accept the Orthodox understanding of marriage?

_____

_____

5. Are you ready to take up the cross of marriage and commit yourself to the ascetic labor of cutting off your own will within the relationship? Can you commit yourself to working to meet your partner's needs rather than your own?

_____

_____

_____

Notes and comments/ things to discuss:

2

WHAT DO YOU EXPECT?

Mary and John sat in my office in complete silence. They had requested to meet with me to talk about their marriage. "Tell me, why are you here?" I questioned.

They looked at each other for a brief moment, and Mary began to speak: "Something has gone wrong, desperately wrong. We don't know what it is, but we can hardly speak to each other without fighting. He's angry with me, and I'm angry with him. And the funny thing is, we don't really know why. Something is wrong, but we can't figure it out."

That they were having problems was no surprise to me. Over the past few months it had become increasingly obvious that there was great tension between them. Things were not good in their relationship.

Such had not always been the case. There was a time not too long before when you couldn't separate them. They were always together and clearly they enjoyed each other's company. Everyone knew that they were deeply in love and were meant for each other. Yet here they were, sitting in my office, barely speaking to each other, angry, bitter, and resentful. And all of this less than a year after their wedding.

As you think about your marriage, I'd like to

"Bless these your servants who by Your providence are united in the communion of marriage. Bless their comings and goings; fill their life with all that is good."
—a prayer from the Orthodox wedding liturgy

Page 31

be able to tell you that Mary and John are an exception and that most marriages don't turn out this way. But I can't! For the sad truth is that many marriages are in exactly the same position as Mary and John's. Not all reach the same point as quickly, but many end up there.

What makes this really sad is that Mary and John really did love each other. When they decided to get married, they did so with the best of motives and with the greatest desire to make their marriage last. And even after they were married, they both worked very hard at the marriage. But something went wrong—something they couldn't explain, something they couldn't fix.

As we began to talk about the first year of their marriage, it became clear to me that the breakdown of the marriage had happened very gradually—indeed, imperceptibly. There was no major moral failure on the part of either John or Mary: no adultery, no drunkenness, no obvious neglect; just little things. Mary was not as interested in sex as John would have liked. John was too interested in watching television and didn't talk as much as Mary would have liked. Mary spent too much time on the phone with her mother. John didn't clean up around the house. All of these were little things. Not one of them was enough to break a marriage. Yet the little things had multiplied to create an atmosphere of bitterness and anger. One wise man said: "Catch us the foxes, the little foxes that spoil the vines" (Song of Solomon 2:15). In Mary and John's case, the little foxes were destroying their marriage.

As you think seriously about your marriage, it is very important that you learn from the example of Mary and John. How do you catch the little foxes and keep them from ruining your vineyard with its ripe grapes? Let me suggest a few things for you to consider.

First, Mary and John got married with a set

of expectations for the marriage and for each other. Sadly, most of these expectations were unspoken and in many cases, even unknown to the one who had them. But the expectations were the standard by which they judged the marriage, themselves, and each other. Almost all of their marital strife could be traced back to this source.

For example, in Mary's family, her father took great responsibility for the physical structure of the house and worked hard to keep it in good repair. This shaped Mary's expectations of her husband-to-be: "A good husband fixes the house when it needs fixing; a good husband is proactive in taking care of things; a good husband doesn't need to be asked to do things, he just does them." John, however, grew up in a family where Dad basically did nothing around the house without being asked and cajoled by Mom. Things were often allowed to deteriorate before they were fixed. His expectations of himself as a husband, therefore, certainly did not equal Mary's.

During their courtship this wasn't a problem, but after they got married and moved into their home, it became a real issue. As things deteriorated, John didn't do anything to fix them. "If it bothers her, she'll ask," he thought. "That is what my mother always did." Mary, however, didn't ask him to fix things. "A good husband doesn't need to be asked, and a good wife never nags." As things broke down and remained unfixed, Mary began to grow bitter: "Why doesn't he fix the shower? That window has been busted for weeks. Doesn't he love me? What kind of lazy man did I marry?" John certainly sensed Mary's bitterness and disapproval but didn't know what he had done or was doing wrong. The tension was there, but because he didn't know why, he couldn't do anything about it.

On the other hand, John entered marriage expecting it to be very erotic. As he was growing

> "Tell my sisters to love the Lord and be satisfied with their husbands in flesh and spirit. In the same way tell my brothers in the name of Jesus Christ to love their wives as the Lord does the Church."
> —St. Ignatius of Antioch

up, he envisioned marriage to be very sexual in expression. In his dreams about the future, his wife would meet him at the door dressed in a scanty nightgown and escort him to the bedroom. His wife would be very sexually active and would fulfill his every fantasy. Mary, however, had grown up with a different set of expectations. It never crossed her mind to meet him at the door, let alone to be dressed immodestly. After all, what if the neighbors saw her? She was interested in sex, but not every night. Sadly, they never talked about this. But night after night, as John came home to find Mary in normal clothes, he began to grow bitter: "Why doesn't she. . .? If she loved me, she would . . . If she were a good wife, she would . . ." His unspoken expectations became the standard by which Mary was judged. Mary, of course, was aware of John's anger and disapproval. But she didn't know why he was so displeased. She couldn't understand why he was always in such a bad mood when he came home from work. Gradually, she began to grow bitter and resentful. "I deserve better treatment than this. After all, I work too. What kind of husband is sullen every night when he comes home from work?"

Saint Paul warns us to look carefully in our relationships "lest any root of bitterness springing up cause trouble" (Hebrews 12:15). In Mary and John's marriage, bitterness had taken root and was causing deep trouble. Bitterness is so dangerous because it clouds our entire vision. As we grow more and more bitter, we become more and more obsessed with the negative. Soon all we can see is the other person's failures. Soon we are filled with anger, and so is our marriage.

Thus, as Mary, John, and I worked through the issues, we struggled to find the reason for their bitterness. We discovered each one's unspoken expectations of the other to be the root cause. Each had to realize that it was unfair to judge the other by standards which were not known.

Furthermore, the more we talked about these standards and expectations, the more they both realized that they had to be willing to change their expectations. For a host of reasons, Mary would never be the erotic wife of John's dreams. And, for another set of reasons, John would never be the fix-it-up man of Mary's dreams. For their marriage to work, each person had to be willing to sacrifice his or her own dreams and accept the other person as he/she was! Without this willingness to communicate and to sacrifice, their marriage was doomed to failure.

The lesson for you is the same, whether you are preparing for marriage or have been married a long time. Whether you are aware of it or not, you have certain expectations. You judge yourself, your partner, and your marriage on the basis of these expectations. The more you can clarify and express them, the better able you and your partner will be to understand your own sense of disappointment and bitterness. The more you are willing to critique your expectations and change them to match reality, the more able you will be to avoid disappointment and bitterness.

FOR FURTHER READING:

Plain Talk on Marriage
by Fr. Gordon Walker
(Supplement H)

To help you in the process, think about the following questions and be prepared to discuss them. As you are able, jot down your answers.

A) HOW AND WHY DID YOU CHOOSE YOUR PARTNER?
Note to married couples: *Answer the questions in section A in the past tense. How would you have answered them before you were married?*

1. Why do you want to get married?

_____

_____

_____

_____

2. What thoughts does the word "marriage" bring to you?

_____

_____

_____

_____

_____

_____

3. How do you know that this person is the one you should marry? What led you to your decision to marry him/her? Why do you want to marry him/her?

_____

_____

_____

_____

_____

4. What attracts you to this person? Why did you first want to date him/her? Have the reasons for continuing the relationship changed as your relationship has matured?

_____

_____

_____

_____

_____

B) WHAT IS YOUR VIEW OF A GOOD SPOUSE?

5. Finish the following sentences:

a. When I am down and discouraged, a good spouse. . .

b. When he/she is down and discouraged, a good spouse. . .

_____

c. When I am happy, a good spouse. . .

_____

d. When he/she is happy, a good spouse. . .

_____

e. When I am busy, a good spouse. . .

_____

f. When he/she is busy, a good spouse. . .

_____

g. When I am worried, a good spouse. . .

_____

h. When he/she is worried, a good spouse. . .

_____

i. When I am angry, a good spouse. . .

_____

j. When he/she is angry, a good spouse. . .

_____

k. When I am sick, a good spouse. . .

_____

l. When he/she is sick, a good spouse. . .

_____

m. When I have to stay at the office longer than anticipated, a good
spouse. . .

_____

n. When my parents call and/or visit, a good spouse. . .

_____

o. When his/her parents call or visit, a good spouse. . .

_____

p. When finances are tight, a good spouse. . .

_____

q. When my friends come over to visit, a good spouse. . .

_____

r. When his/her friends come over to visit, a good spouse. . .

_____

s. When we have a disagreement, a good spouse. . .

_____

t. When he/she is wrong and fails me, a good spouse. . .

_____

u. When there is a major decision to be made, a good husband. . .

_____

v. When there is a major decision to be made, a good wife. . .

_____

w. When something goes wrong with the house, car, etc., a good wife. . .

_____

x. When something goes wrong with the house, car, etc., a good husband. . .

_____

y. When the house is a mess, a good wife. . .

_____

z. When the house is a mess, a good husband. . .

_____

aa. In the sexual aspect of married life, a good wife. . .

_____

bb. In the sexual aspect of married life, a good husband. . .

_____

6. Compare your expectations with your partner's.

a. Where are there major differences? Discuss the implications of the differences together. Summarize your findings.

_____
_____
_____
_____
_____
_____

b. In what areas are you being unrealistic? On the basis of your knowledge of your partner, what expectations can he/she not meet? Summarize your findings.

_____
_____
_____
_____
_____

c. **(For married couples):** How have your unrealistic expectations of your spouse created problems in your marriage?

_____
_____
_____
_____

MEETING YOUR SPOUSE'S NEEDS

Mary and John both got married looking to the other person to meet their needs and desires. This was abundantly evident from their response to their partner's failures. Their bitterness was an indication of their selfish approach to marriage. For their marriage to be restored, it was necessary for them to change their orientation. Instead of seeing themselves as the served, they had to see themselves as the servers!

Our Lord Himself is the prime example. In the Gospels, several times He gently chides the disciples for their desire to be served, and He holds Himself up as the model: "The Son of Man did not come to be served, but to serve, and to give His life a ransom for many" (Matthew 20:28). In marriage, you must follow Jesus' example. You must get married (and stay married) not to be served, but to serve, and to give your life to and for your partner.

Bishop Kallistos Ware has written: "Egocentricity is the death of true personhood. Each becomes a real person only through entering into relation with other persons, through living for them and in them. . . . Self-love is hell; for, carried to its ultimate conclusion, self-love signifies the end of all joy and all meaning" (*The Orthodox Way,* p. 5). If this is true for us as persons, how much more for the sacred union of two persons in marriage! Saint John of Kronstadt said: "There can be no Church apart from love." Likewise, there can be no marriage apart from love.

In the next chapter, we will discuss at greater length what love means and how it should function in marriage. In this chapter I wish to focus your attention on the all-important truth that, if you desire your marriage to grow in love and joy, you must get married not primarily to receive, but to give. For as Jesus said: "It is more blessed to give than to receive" (Acts 20:35).

Additional note for married couples:

Throughout this chapter we have been talking about the need to develop selflessness in our marriages. You know how difficult it really is! After the initial excitement wears off and the honeymoon is over, the hard work of making a marriage begins. Selfishness—the desire to have things my way in order to make me happy—is a passion all we less-than-perfect human beings must struggle with. Undoubtedly, you and your spouse have experienced the reality of this struggle in your own relationship. As you answer the questions listed below, be humble enough to admit your own mistakes and your own failings. Both of you have them! There can be no finger-pointing here because both partners are guilty. What there can be, however, is repentance. And understand, repentance is not a negative thing where we beat on ourselves and make ourselves "pay" for the mistakes of the past. Repentance is rather a glorious opportunity to see ourselves as we really are, to admit our mistakes and failings, and to reorient ourselves to the fulfilling of Christ's commandments and to the deeper experience of His liberating love. As you answer the following questions, please don't selfishly look for opportunities to score points with your spouse. Rather, look for ways to humble yourself before your spouse and ask his or her forgiveness. Remember: God does not dwell with the one who justifies himself, but with the one who prays: "Have mercy on me, a sinner."

As you think about meeting your spouse's needs, answer the following questions:

1. If you were asked to describe your relationship in one word, what would that word be? _____

2. What word would your partner use? _____

3. What are some of the strong points of your relationship?

_____

_____

4. What are some of the weak points of your relationship?

_____

_____

5. What have you done to strengthen the weak points?

_____

_____

6. What do you bring to the marriage to make it a success?

_____

_____

7. What needs in your partner's life has God gifted you to meet?

_____

_____

8. How is your partner a better person because he/she knows you?

_____

_____

9. How will your partner be a better person ten years from now
   because he/she is married to you?

_____

_____

Notes and comments/ things to discuss:

◯◯◯

3

HOW DO YOU SAY "I LOVE YOU"

"Though I speak with the tongues of men and of angels, but have not love, I have become as sounding brass or a clanging cymbal. And though I have the gift of prophecy, and understand all mysteries and all knowledge, and though I have all faith, so that I could remove mountains, but have not love, I am nothing. . . . And now abide faith, hope, love, these three; but the greatest of these is love" (1 Corinthians 13:1, 2, 13).

With these very beautiful and poetic words, Saint Paul reminds us of the importance of love. Without love we are nothing. Without love we are less than human. Mother Maria of Paris summarizes the biblical understanding: "However hard I try, I find it impossible to construct anything greater than these three words, 'Love one another' —only to the end, and without exceptions: then all is justified and life is illumined, whereas otherwise it is an abomination and a burden." In an Orthodox perspective, the importance of love cannot be overstressed.

Our understanding of the Trinity highlights this. Saint John says: "God is love" (1 John 4:16). According to the tenets of the Orthodox Faith, the one true God exists eternally as three distinct Persons: Father, Son, and Holy Spirit. This

Marital love is "a thing that no possession can equal; for nothing, nothing whatever [apart from heavenly good things], is more precious than to be loved by a wife and to love her."
—St. John Chrysostom

theological truth reveals something very important about what it means to be a person. No one exists by himself! To be a person is to live, and to live is to love. Not even God exists alone; He exists eternally in a relationship of love. No marriage can last the test of time, no marriage can endure the storms of life, unless it is first and foremost a relationship of love.

The Church teaches that marriage is a sacrament. God gives special grace to those who enter into a marriage which is blessed by the Church. But we would be wrong to think of this grace as some sort of magic or automatic guarantee. Like all grace, the grace of marriage must be received and it must be lived. Grace can be resisted! This is as true of marriage as it is of every other sacrament.

How do we resist the grace given to us in our marriages? Whenever we cease loving our spouse. How do we cooperate with the grace which has been given? By loving our spouse.

Dr. Peter Kallelis explains: "For believing Christians, matrimony is a sacrament, a visible sign of God's invisible grace and of His presence in our lives. Practical consequences flow from the sacramental nature of marriage. If the sign of the sacrament is this promise and this living out of the promise, then it follows that every time you are faithful, tender, considerate, every time you compromise or reconcile, every time you are thoughtful or unselfish, God's grace enters your lives. Each time, Christ becomes present in your midst; each time, the Holy Spirit dwells in your heart and in your home" (*Holy Matrimony,* p. 16).

Father Theoklitos of Dionysiou confirms this belief: "There is one truth that reigns supreme from the fringes of the throne of glory down to the least shadow of the most insignificant of creatures: and that one truth is love. Love is the source from which the holy streams of grace flow down unceasingly from the city of God, watering the earth and making it fruitful. . . . It is love that fashions all things and holds them in unity. It is love that gives life and warmth, that inspires and guides. Love is the seal set upon creation, the signature of the Creator. Love is the explanation of His handiwork. How can we make Christ come and dwell in our hearts? How else, except through love?"

For your marriage to last, for you to be fulfilled in and by your sacramental union, for your marriage to be an icon of Christ to the world, you must love one another. Without love your marriage will be nothing more than a sounding brass and a clanging cymbal. With love your marriage can and will be filled with joy, peace, and the presence of Christ Himself.

But what is love? Very few today would deny the importance of love for a successful marriage. But not all agree on a definition of love. For some, love is an emotional high; for others, love is exclusively proper behavior.

WHAT IS LOVE?

The best definition ever was given by Saint Paul in 1 Corinthians chapter 13 (see right column).

It is interesting to me that the great Apostle does not so much define love as illustrate it. His is no rational definition, but rather a superabundance of description. Saint John Chrysostom exhorts us: "But do not thou hastily pass by, beloved, the things spoken, but examine each one of them with much care, that thou mayest know both the treasure which is in the thing and the art of the painter" (Homily 33, Volume 12, *Nicene and Post-Nicene Fathers*).

As we examine each line we learn more of the Spirit of love. Look again at each description. Try to explain in your words what is being said

"Love suffers long and is kind; love does not envy; love does not parade itself, is not puffed up; does not behave rudely, does not seek its own, is not provoked, thinks no evil; does not rejoice in iniquity, but rejoices in the truth; bears all things, believes all things, hopes all things, endures all things. Love never fails."
—1 Corinthians 13:4–8

about love. Then, think about how you can show that aspect of love to your partner. To get you started, let me do the first one for you:

1. Love suffers long.

MEANING: Love is not impatient or nasty. Love is not fretful or intolerant. Love is patient, willing to suffer long without retaliating. Love gives the other person space. Love is willing to wait. Love doesn't manipulate or sinfully pressure the other person into changing.

EXAMPLE: When my partner doesn't see things the way I see them, loving him or her means I will not try to coerce agreement with me by the loudness of my voice, or by threats, or by being critical or silent, or by withdrawing. Love means that I will allow my partner to think differently. I will not attempt to overpower or force conforming to me. (This example first appeared in *Preparing for Marriage* by Wayne Mack, p. 22).

Work through the following descriptions on your own. (NOTE: You may want to redo the first using examples more appropriate to your own relationship.)

1. Love is kind.

MEANING:_____

_____

_____

EXAMPLES:_____

_____

_____

_____

2. Love does not envy.

MEANING:_____

_____

_____

EXAMPLES:_____

_____

_____

_____

3. Love does not parade itself, is not puffed up.

MEANING:_____

_____

_____

EXAMPLES:_____

_____

_____

_____

4. Love does not behave rudely.

MEANING:_____

_____

_____

EXAMPLES:_____

_____

_____

_____

5. Love does not seek its own.

MEANING:_____

_____

_____

EXAMPLES:_____

_____

_____

_____

6. Love is not easily provoked.

MEANING:_____

_____

_____

EXAMPLES:_____

_____

_____

_____

7. Love thinks no evil.

MEANING:_____

_____

_____

EXAMPLES:_____

_____

_____

_____

8. Love does not rejoice in iniquity, but rejoices in the truth.

MEANING:_____

_____

_____

EXAMPLES:_____

_____

_____

_____

9. Love bears all things, believes all things, hopes all things, endures all things. Love never fails.

MEANING:_____

_____

_____

EXAMPLES:_____

_____

_____

_____

BREAKDOWNS IN SHOWING LOVE

Now that you have a good handle on the importance of love and a general understanding of its meaning for your relationship, we can move on to another consideration. Almost every couple I know has gotten married for one simple reason: they love each other. I have yet to hear someone tell me that they got married for another reason. And I believe that the vast majority of those who claim to marry for love really do try to love their partner. But as you well know, not all of these marriages survive. Many end in divorce. What happens?

In some instances, one or both of the partners stops loving the other. But in many marriages this is not the case. Both partners really are trying to love the other person, but the marriage still doesn't make it. Why?

Many marital failures are caused by a misunderstanding of the nature of love. For a multitude of reasons (nature, nurture, and a combination of the two) we all develop what I call "love sensors."

Love sensors are the way we receive love from others. Each person has a slightly different set of love sensors. For some, love is primarily received through physical affection. When these people want to be shown love, they want to be hugged, kissed, and caressed. Others receive love through verbal support. When these people want to be shown love, they want to be encouraged, affirmed, and/or comforted. Still others experience love through physical actions. When these people want to be shown love, they want the house to be cleaned, the car to be washed, the lawn to be mowed, etc. Others receive love through gifts and special presents. When they want to be shown love, they want a special gift or present to be given. Still others receive love through companionship. When they want to be loved, they just want to spend time with the other person.

It is significant to note that every person is different and receives love in his own unique way. As human beings made in the image of God, each of us has our own unique personality, unique traits which set us apart from everyone else. Part of our uniqueness is the way we receive love. In some respects we're all the same. In others we are vastly different one from another.

Furthermore, it is also highly important to realize that we have a tendency to assume that other people receive love the way we receive love. Theologically speaking, this is a manifestation of egocentricity. It is difficult for us to move out beyond ourselves and to know others as unique persons. In a sad perversion of humanity, we tend to export our persons onto others and deny them their own freedom to be the persons God made them to be.

Now, in marriage this produces tremendous havoc. For example, let's say that Sally's love sensor is very attuned to companionship and communication. When she wants to feel loved, she wants Hank to sit down and talk to her and hold her and spend great amounts of time doing nothing but being with her. Hank, on the other hand, is very attuned to receiving love through helping, through working hard, through fixing the house, etc. The problem is that Sally doesn't receive love that way. So no matter how hard Hank tries to show Sally he loves her, she still feels that he doesn't. For every time Hank gets juiced up to show Sally love, he goes out and does something. He fixes the sink, he mows the lawn, he washes the car, etc. Notice that all of these things actually take him away from Sally. To accomplish these things he must leave Sally alone. But for Sally, if someone loves you they spend time with you. So she receives Hank's attempts to show love as manifestations of a lack of love. Therefore, the irony of the situation is that the more Hank tries to show Sally he loves her, the more she feels unloved!

On the other hand, when Sally wants to show Hank she loves him, she stops cleaning the house, making the dinner, etc., and comes and sits next to him and tries to talk to him. Hank sees this as an expression not of love but of careless neglect. So, the more Sally tries to show Hank she loves him, the more unloved he feels.

There is only way to break this cycle. And that is the way of divine love. Divine love begins by assessing the capacity of the person to be loved to receive love. Divine love seeks to find the "love sensors" of the person, and then it dedicates itself to showing love in a way that the person will understand and receive it. This is the wonder of the Incarnation. Christ became man; He assumed

"Show her, too, that you set a high value on her company, and that you are more desirous to be at home for her sake, than in the market-place. And esteem her before all your friends, and above the children that are born of her, and let these very children be beloved by thee for her sake. If she does any good act, praise and admire it."
—St. John Chrysostom

the fullness of our own humanity. He became as we are, excepting only sin, to show us His love. Instead of demanding that we change the way we receive love, He changed the way He showed love. "For God so loved the world that He gave His only begotten Son" (John 3:16). Love in our marriages demands that we do the same.

We must learn to show love the way our partner receives love. Furthermore, we must learn to receive love the way our partner shows love. This is what Saint John of Kronstadt means when he says: "Look at every human being as if he were unique in God's world, a great miracle of God's wisdom and grace, and do not let the fact that you are accustomed to him serve as a ground for neglect" (Bishop Alexander, *The Life of Father John of Kronstadt,* p. 126).

Your partner is a unique individual. There is no one on earth like him or her. Your job—your mission—is to know him/her in all of his/her uniqueness and show the love of Christ to him/her in the context of the wonder of his/her uniqueness. Don't demand that he or she change to meet you. Rather, you change to meet him or her! "Let each of you look out not only for his own interests, but also for the interests of others" (Philippians 2:4).

1. To help you understand yourself better and to isolate your "love sensors," fill in the following sentences:

a. When I was a child, I knew my parents loved me because they . . .

_____

_____

b. When I was a child, I knew my parents loved each other, because they . . .

_____

_____

c. When I really want to show love to my partner I . . .

_____

_____

d. When I am discouraged I want my partner to . . .

_____

_____

e. After a disagreement I want my partner to . . .

_____

_____

f. I feel secure when my partner . . .

_____

_____

g. I have strong affectionate feelings when my partner . . .

_____

_____

h. I wish my partner would more frequently . . .

_____

_____

2. Compare your answers to question one with your partner's. Discuss areas of possible misunderstanding.

_____

_____

_____

_____

_____

_____

_____

_____

3. In his book, *How Do You Say I Love You?* Judson Swihart isolates seven different ways of receiving love. Look over the following list adapted from his book and rate them (1 being the most important, 7 being the least) in terms of how **you** receive love.

[ ]   a. Helping (i.e., doing fix-it jobs, taking care of material possessions)

[ ]   b. Companionship (i.e., spending time together, being there, doing things together, being willing to communicate)

[ ]   c. Solicitude (i.e., being concerned about opinions, feelings, interests, desires, likes, dislikes; listening, sharing, being cooperative)

[ ]   d. Physical affection

[ ]   e. Communication (i.e., saying it with words, expressing appreciation and admiration)

[ ]   f. Faithfulness (i.e., being loyal, trustworthy, supportive, unselfish, responsible, keeping confidences, fulfilling promises and commitments)

[ ]   g. Gift-giving (i.e. doing extra, beyond the call of duty, things like giving special gifts, cards, flowers, etc.)

4. Now that you have isolated your own "love sensors," think about your partner. How does he/she receive love? Rate these indicators (1 being the most important, 7 being the least) in terms of how your partner receives love (answer the questions as you believe **your partner** would answer them).

[ ]   a. Helping (i.e., doing fix-it jobs, taking care of material possessions)

[ ]   b. Companionship (i.e., spending time together, being there, doing things together, being willing to communicate)

[ ]   c. Solicitude (i.e., being concerned about opinions, feelings, interests, desires, likes, dislikes; listening, sharing, being cooperative)

[ ]   d. Physical affection

[ ]   e. Communication (i.e., saying it with words, expressing appreciation and admiration)

[ ]   f. Faithfulness (i.e., being loyal, trustworthy, supportive, unselfish, responsible, keeping confidences, fulfilling promises and commitments)

[ ]   g. Gift-giving (i.e. doing extra, beyond the call of duty, things like giving special gifts, cards, flowers, etc.)

How is your partner different from you? How can you show love more appropriately? Summarize your thinking.

_____

_____

_____

5. Make a list of the appropriate longings and desires of your partner. Think of his/her total life. What does he/she need and/ or want in each one of these areas? How can you begin to meet his/her needs and fulfill his/her desires? Be specific.

a. Physical needs

_____

_____

_____

b. Emotional needs

_____

_____

_____

c. Spiritual needs

_____

_____

_____

d. Intellectual needs

_____

_____

_____

e. Financial needs

_____

_____

_____

f. Other needs

_____

_____

_____

6. **(For married couples):** Have your differing "love sensors" caused problems in your marriage?

_____

_____

_____

Notes and comments/ things to discuss:

⚭⚭

4

LEAVING AND CLEAVING

"Why doesn't my mother like my husband? All she does is speak negatively about him and criticize everything he does. It wasn't always that way. When we first got married she really liked him. But now after three years of marriage she can't stand him. I feel like I'm getting torn in two. I love my mother but I also love my husband. Tell me, Father, what can I do?"

The woman sitting in my office was in tears. It was obvious that the emotional strain was wearing her down. Janet felt forced to choose between two people she loved dearly. And she was deeply hurting, as was her relationship with Tom, her husband.

What happened? Why did her mother turn on her husband? This is the issue we explored together. As we talked it became clear that the root of the problem went back to the early days of their marriage. When Janet and Tom were first married things were rocky. They both had lived independent lives before marriage, and it took some time for them to adjust to a married life-style. Sadly, during this rocky time, Janet had turned to her mother for comfort.

Whenever Tom did something selfish or hurt her, she would call her mother and complain about Tom. Her mother, out of motherly love, always took her side and commiserated with

> "Therefore a man shall leave his father and mother and be joined to his wife, and they shall become one flesh."
> —Genesis 2:24

Page 57

her. This lasted for almost a year and a half.

Gradually, however, as Tom and Janet worked at their marriage, the problems began to be less severe, and both of them adapted to each other and to their married state. Janet's complaints became less severe, and her calls to her mother less frequent.

Her mother wasn't sure she liked the new arrangement. She didn't understand what had happened to their close relationship. She blamed Tom. Of course, this was to be expected. First, she had listened for a year and a half to Janet's complaints and criticisms of Tom. Janet had taught her mother to think negatively about Tom. Second, her close relationship with her daughter after Janet's marriage had been completely built around complaining about Tom. Without either of them being aware of it, they had established their relationship on a negative basis. Thus, as Janet's mother felt her relationship with her daughter sliding away, it was natural for her to try to reestablish the relationship on the basis of negativity. They had been drawn together by a mutual dislike. It had become the emotional glue which kept them together. Without being aware of it, Janet's mother was trying desperately (out of fear of losing her daughter) to reapply the glue.

I share this story with you because it illustrates the importance of this chapter. It is fun to joke about "mothers-in-law," but in reality, when the rubber meets the road in your marriage, your relationship with your in-laws will be no laughing matter. It is important to think through the issues which are involved, lest you find yourself in a mess as Janet did a couple of years down the road.

In Genesis 2:24, immediately after the record of the woman being brought to the man, we read: "Therefore a man shall leave his father and mother and be joined to his wife, and they shall become one flesh." This passage is so important that our Lord Himself quotes it in a dialogue with the Pharisees (see Matthew 19:1-6). Two important actions are highlighted here. Both are necessary for a fulfilled and fulfilling marriage.

Dr. Kallelis explains: "The marriage means . . . the final cutting of the emotional umbilical cord, a total release from the family womb. . . . It signifies the time of dependence upon parents has ended (although this independence may have started sometime earlier), and the period of interdependence of the partners has begun" (*Holy Matrimony*, p. 9).

LEAVING THE OLD BEHIND

First, the new couple is instructed to leave their parents, signifying that the time of dependence has ended. The concern here is not so much geographical as it is emotional. Children grow up in an environment almost completely shaped by their parents. Much of what they learn during the formative years of their lives they learn directly from their parents. Their lives are parent-centered and parent-controlled. This is even true of those who rebel in their teenage years. What they do or don't do still very much revolves around who their parents are and what they expect.

When a couple gets married, they must leave this parent-centered, parent-controlled life-style behind. This certainly does not mean that you abandon or utterly forsake your parents. No, they will always be your parents. Your relationship with them will always be important and should always be filled with deep and abiding love.

But what it does mean is that you must establish an adult relationship with them. No longer should their concerns, their ideas, and their desires be the primary concern in your decision making. No longer should their love and acceptance be most important. In short, you must work to

" 'For this reason a man shall leave his father and mother and be joined to his wife, and the two shall become one flesh'; so then they are no longer two, but one flesh. Therefore what God has joined together, let no man separate."
—Mark 7:9

make your relationship with your spouse the *priority* relationship in your life. For "the beginning of a new existence together with the one we love means facing life as it is, sharing joys with one another, and sorrows as well. There should be no turning back now, no clinging to childhood or adolescent crutches" (Kallelis, *Holy Matrimony,* p. 9).

It is especially important that you establish this kind of relationship when you experience problems in your marriage. Janet learned the hard way that running to Mom or Dad when things are hard establishes destructive patterns. Once again, this is more difficult than at first it seems. Believe it or not, after so many years of going to Mom and Dad with your hurts and sorrows, it is hard to break the habit. When things get rough, you almost instinctively will want to run home and be comforted by Mom and Dad. For the good of your marriage, you must resist this temptation.

A NEW UNION

But leaving your parents and a dependent lifestyle is not enough. Secondly, a healthy marriage requires the new couple to be joined to one another, to be interdependent on each other. In this we are reminded that marriage is a lifelong commitment two people make before God to each other. In my first parish I was an assistant to a pastor who had been in ministry for over forty years. He had an interesting routine which he went through before every marriage ceremony. He would take the man to the back of the church and show him the back door. And then he would say: "Use it now if you want to. But once you've been married, consider this door permanently closed!"

To be joined to one another, however, means more than simply staying married. I know lots of couples who have stayed married who are not "joined." Their marriage is a static coexistence of two people who live in the same house and sleep in the same bed. They are like plants which are in the same garden. They are together, but they are not joined. To be joined is a dynamic concept; it implies the sharing of life. The image is not that of two separate plants side by side, but that of two plants which have been grafted together. To use Jesus' words, to be joined is to be "no longer two but one" (Matthew 19:6).

When you are married, God wishes you and your spouse to share all things with each other. Just as salvation in an Orthodox perspective is sharing all that I am with all that God is, so marriage in an Orthodox perspective is sharing all that I am with all that my wife is. Marriage is not only the union of two bodies in sexual intercourse, but also the union of two wills, two hearts, two lives.

Probably the greatest example of marital union is to be found in the grandparents of God, Saints Joachim and Anna. The Church tells us that they were "two bodies possessing one soul and mind" (Monk Moses, *Married Saints of the Church,* p. 110). Although severely tested by the infertility of Anna's womb, they never wavered in their faith nor in their love for one another. Their holy icon is a gracious picture of true marital happiness. As they stand before their house they embrace. If you examine the icon closely, you will discover that their embrace is so intimate and their union so complete that they stand not as two but as one. This is God's design and desire for marriage: two individuals with two different backgrounds and personalities sharing a new life together, and thus becoming one.

Notice I said a "new" life together. To be thoroughly joined to each other, it is necessary for the two of you to be willing to change—to develop new ways of doing things. Your relationship will certainly reflect who the two of you were before you were married. It is very important for you to understand each other's pasts—your unique upbringing and family's life-style—in order to understand each other's unspoken expectations about marriage and married life. Your marriage will reflect "something old." But, at the same time, it must be something new. It must be the unique and exciting development of new ways of doing things, new habits, and new patterns!

Ultimately, this represents both the challenge and the wonder of marriage. Your marriage can be likened to new wine. Therefore, make sure you put it into new wineskins. For, if you do not, the old wineskins will burst, the wine will be spilled, and the wineskins ruined (see Mark 2:22). But if you do put the new wine into new wineskins, as each year passes, the wine will mature and deepen; each year will heighten the rich flavors of your unique blend!

Additional note for married couples:

In-law problems! Chances are that you have had them. And chances are, some of the most intense moments of your married life have revolved around your relationship with the extended family. As you look through the following questions, please refrain from pointing the finger at each other. It is so easy to do, but so damaging once it is done. **Most of the questions will be appropriate to you. Some of them will have to be answered in the past tense rather than the present. Please don't skip the hard work of looking back and thinking through your relationship with your parents. This is a good thing for you.** For true marital unity to come about, it is necessary that spouses be honest both with themselves and with each other. Out of this honesty can come true understanding. And out of understanding can come deep, intense unity and communion. Many of these issues you discuss will not fall into the "right versus wrong" category. Different does not always mean wrong. Sometimes it just means different. Understanding differences without being threatened by them or demanding that the other spouse change just to meet our expectations is an important aspect of a fulfilling marriage.

Additional note for engaged couples:

The time around the wedding is not easy for anyone. It is difficult for parents, who watch their beloved son or daughter leave; it is difficult for children, who leave the protective shield of their parents and embark on a new adventure. It is a time of transition.

It is crucial that you talk with your parents *before* you are married about the kind of relationship you now have, and the kind of relationship you desire to have with them after the marriage. If there are serious relationship problems with your parents, try to resolve them before your marriage. It is hard enough to build a strong marriage. Don't bring the hurts of the past with you. Deal with them as best you can and put them behind you.

To help you think more deeply about the issues raised in this chapter, think through the following questions, jotting down your responses.

1. Do you have any unresolved problems with your own parents? Are there hurts from the past which have not been settled? Do you need to confess any failings to them?

_____

_____

_____

_____

_____

_____

2. Before you get married, what do you need to do in order to start your marriage with a clean slate?

_____

_____

_____

_____

_____

3. What kind of relationship did you have with your parents as you were growing up? In what ways was your life centered around them? In what ways was your life controlled by them?

_____

_____

_____

_____

_____

4. As you have moved into adulthood, how has your relationship with your parents changed? In what ways does your life still center around them? In what ways is your life still controlled by them?

_____

_____

_____

_____

_____

5. What kind of relationship do you envision having with your parents after you are married? Try to be specific in your thinking.

_____

_____

_____

_____

_____

6. What problem areas do you see in your relationship with your parents? What will be the hardest area? In what aspects will it be difficult for you to fully leave your parents?

_____

_____

_____

_____

_____

7. How do your parents feel about your plans for marriage?

_____

_____

_____

_____

_____

8. Describe your partner's relationship with his/her parents.

_____

_____

_____

_____

_____

9. What problem areas do you see in your partner's relationship with his/her parents? How and in what areas will it be difficult for your partner to leave his/her parents?

_____

_____

_____

_____

_____

10. What kind of relationship do you currently have with your in-laws? How do you think your in-laws view you?

_____

_____

_____

_____

_____

11. What kind of relationship do you envision having with your in-laws? What would you consider to be "interfering" by your in-laws?

_____

_____

_____

_____

_____

12. How are you going to handle holidays, feast days, and the like? Describe how you would like to spend your first Thanksgiving, Christmas, and Pascha.

_____

_____

_____

_____

_____

13. Describe your parents' relationship with their parents. How has this shaped your own perspective and your own expectations?

_____

_____

_____

_____

Additional note for engaged couples:

Now that you have thought through these issues on your own, schedule some time with your partner before your next meeting with your priest to talk them through. Be honest with each other about your concerns, fears, and desires. It may very well be that you will have some serious differences of opinion on these issues. That is okay. Talk them through. Don't allow yourself to get angry or bitter. Understand what your partner is saying before you criticize, disagree, or attack. If there are some issues you can't resolve, make sure you talk about them with your priest.

Note to engaged couples, continued:

After the two of you have reached an agreement (which may happen before or after your next session), it is very important that you talk to both sets of parents. Ask them questions before you tell them what you think. Find out what they envision your relationship with them to be like after the marriage. Talk to them about the possible pitfalls; discuss freely and openly how you are going to work together to avoid them. Although it is not always achievable, the more open communication you can have on these issues, the less chance there is that deep hurts will develop after the wedding.

14. It is also important that you and your partner come together and discuss the differences and similarities between your families. Make sure you answer the following questions. Jot down any major differences you uncover.

a. How would you rate the marriage of your parents (good, fair, poor, bad; still together, divorced, separated, etc.)?

_____

_____

b. How did your parents relate to each other? What were their respective views on the responsibilities of husbands and wives and fathers and mothers? How were major decisions made in your families?

_____

_____

_____

_____

_____

c. How did your parents fight? How did they resolve their conflicts?

_____

_____

Page 67

_____

_____

_____

d. What were the fundamental values of your family as you were
   growing up ("cleanliness is next to godliness," "children should
   be seen but not heard," etc.)?

_____

_____

_____

e. What were the fundamental rules of the family ("children should
   not argue with their parents," "your room must always be
   cleaned," etc.)?

_____

_____

_____

f. How did your family handle money? What were the basic beliefs
   about the way finances should be controlled (how money
   should be saved, spent, etc.)?

_____

_____

_____

_____

g. How did your family approach sexual issues (often discussed,
   never discussed, etc.)? How was physical affection expressed
   by your parents in different situations?

_____

_____

_____

_____

h. How open was your family about family matters and/or secrets to outsiders?

_____

_____

i. How involved were your parents in outside activities? Did they always do everything together, did they often do things separately, or was there a mix of the two?

_____

_____

_____

_____

j. What were the expectations your parents had for the children ("attend college," "be involved in athletics," "talk to mom about everything," etc.)?

_____

_____

_____

_____

k. How involved were your parents in the life of the Church? Did your parents have prayer times with the children? Did your parents teach you about God?

_____

_____

_____

_____

15. Now that you have discussed these questions, summarize your findings in response to the following:

a. How are your families of origin alike and how are they different? Write down the major differences you observed.

alike:_____

_____
_____
_____
_____

different:_____
_____
_____
_____
_____

b. How are your mothers and fathers alike and different?

_____
_____
_____
_____
_____
_____

c. **(For engaged couples:)** How may your marriage be affected by these differences?

_____
_____
_____
_____
_____
_____

d. **(For married couples:)** How has your marriage been affected by these differences in family background?

_____
_____
_____

_____

_____

_____

_____

_____

16. Before you finish this chapter, I would like you to think about one more thing. Does either of you sense that there are areas of the other person's life that are being kept from you? Is there anything which is hindering your sharing your life together? For example, does either of you have secrets that you have not shared with the other?

_____

_____

_____

_____

_____

_____

_____

COMING CLEAN

I know that this is a very sensitive subject, and I do not believe that everything from the past needs to be told in the present. I also know that there is no easy formula to follow. As Dr. Kallelis comments: "Determining what of the past to confide and how to do it are hard, often agonizing decisions for any man or woman in love. Both wish to be truly honest and hold nothing back. Yet can he, she accept these confessions? Some persons simply are not strong enough to do so. Is he? Is she? Ultimately, each individual must decide alone. He or she must weigh the past, the partner, the potential harm or benefit such trusting revelations hold for the future. Nevertheless, it should be evident that to blurt out all without consideration is at once naive and unwise" (*Holy Matrimony,* p. 23).

My concern is simply this: that there be no obstacles from the past which will hinder your growing into union with each other in your marriage.

Additional note for engaged couples:

You must be honest with yourself and with your partner, and most importantly with God. Thus I strongly urge you to schedule a time for confession prior to your wedding. At that confession come completely clean before Christ so that you may enter into marriage with no emotional or spiritual baggage from the past.

Notes and comments/ things to discuss:

5

REAL COMMUNICATION

"Wait a minute!" Joyce sat right up in her chair and looked directly at her husband. "You may think that everything's fine between us. But the truth of the matter is that we haven't really communicated in years!"

"What do you mean?" Richard looked astonished. "We talk all the time."

"No," Joyce responded. "You talk all the time. I just listen!"

Communication in marriage! Counselors report that 85 out of every 100 couples seeking marriage counseling list poor communication as a major source of marital strife. For a relationship to develop and grow, it is absolutely essential that the couple know how to communicate.

For us as Orthodox Christians, this emphasis on communication is underscored by our tradition's emphasis on the importance of prayer. The relationship with God which has been given to us must be maintained through communication. Vasilii Rozanov explains the Orthodox understanding: "There is no life without prayer. Without prayer there is only madness and horror" (quoted by Ware, *The Orthodox Way,* p. 140).

Our spiritual life, graciously given to us in and through the sacraments of baptism and chrismation, must be maintained through regular

> "A word fitly spoken is like apples of gold in settings of silver."
> —Proverbs 25:11

communication with God. Salvation in an Orthodox understanding is dynamic and living. "The Christian message of salvation can best be summed up in terms of sharing, of solidarity and identification" (Ware, p. 97). Therefore, we must develop and maintain a relationship with God in which we share with Him and He with us.

This consideration helps us by pointing out not only the importance of communication, but also its real essence. Communication is more than talking. As Richard found out, to really communicate we must do more than flap our lips continuously. Communication is listening, it is understanding, it is sharing. It involves words, but it goes beyond words to the heart!

THREE LEVELS OF COMMUNICATION

To understand this, let's think for a minute about the Orthodox approach to prayer. The great saints of God tell us that there are different levels of prayer. The first level is exclusively verbal. It consists primarily of asking God for things. It is not continuous but sporadic, and is exercised as the need arises. The second level of prayer is deeper, and although it may employ words, is not necessarily dependent on them. To pray in this way is to "*stand before God,* to enter into an immediate and personal relationship with him; it is to know at every level of our being, from the instinctive to the intellectual, from the sub- to the supra-conscious, that we are in God and he is in us" (Elizabeth Behr-Sigel, *The Place of the Heart,* p. 136). According to this definition, prayer is a continuous state of the heart; an abiding awareness of God's presence and of our desire and need for Him. The communication at this level transcends words and certainly far exceeds requests, and dwells in the heart. It is ultimately the sharing of my deep feelings for God with Him.

Notice that both of these levels of prayer are

active. In each level, I take the initiative; I share with God. I communicate with Him and I talk to Him. As we approach the third level, we move beyond our initiative to God's. Saint Gregory of Sinai (fourteenth century) explains: "Why speak at length? Prayer is God, who works all things in all men." Bishop Ware explains: "True inner prayer is to stop talking and to listen to the wordless voice of God within our heart; it is to cease doing things on our own, and to enter into the action of God" (ibid., p. 137). Properly understood, in the Orthodox Tradition, the highest expression of prayer is silence; not my sharing with God, but His sharing with me.

It is very interesting to take these three levels and apply them to our understanding of communication in marriage. The first level of communication is exclusively verbal. If you think back to your first date, most, if not all, of your communication took place on this level. You shared facts and figures with each other: what you like to do, where you've been, what you've done, etc.

As your relationship has developed, hopefully your communication has moved past this level and entered into the second level. (Sadly, not all relationships do!) Now I trust you have begun to share yourselves with each other: who you are, what you feel, etc. At this level, communication is more than verbal. As you have grown to know each other more deeply, you have developed your own ways of communicating feelings and emotions. A gentle touch, a pat on the back, a massaging of the shoulders, a knowing wink . . . all of these become a "secret code" by which you share with each other. If you have reached this level of communication, you have grown comfortable with silence. In a mystical way, somehow you are able to communicate without words. Communication is an awareness of your need and desire to be with each other; to develop a mutual life together; to

"Such is the power of love: it embraces, and unites, and fastens together not only those who are present, and near, and visible, but also those who are far distant. And neither length of time, nor separation in space, nor anything else of that kind, can break up and divide in pieces the affection of the soul."
—St. John Chrysostom

become one in thought, word, emotion, action, and being.

If your relationship has developed on this level, you probably have begun to experience communication on level three as well. This is a level of communication in which you concentrate not on sharing but on receiving, not so much on hearing as on understanding. When you truly communicate, his/her feelings, desires, longings, etc. become yours. He/she doesn't have to tell you what they are, because in a mystical way you know them, and thus, you know him/her not as he/she presents him/herself, but as he/she really is.

Now, don't misunderstand what I am saying about communication. These three levels all exist in our relationships at the same time. My prayer life involves verbal requests and, most likely, always will (at least in this life). But my verbal requests have been supplemented and fulfilled by an ever-developing relationship with God in which I share myself with Him. And, although in a very small and immature manner, even this sharing has been supplemented and fulfilled by God's sharing with me so that, at times, I feel His love, His sorrow, His joy. In the same way, my communication with my wife still involves the sharing of ideas, requests, opinions, etc. But this has been deepened into a sharing of feelings, passions, desires, longings, etc. And the more we have opened ourselves to each other, the more we have grown to feel with the other person, to share not only the concepts and the feelings, but to actually share our persons one with another.

Sadly, many Christians barely move past level one in their prayer life. Sadly, many couples barely move past level one in their marriages. Like Joyce and Richard, although they have never stopped talking, they stopped communicating years ago. My greatest fear is that this might happen to you. Now, if you work at it and keep your commitments, your marriage can last without communication on levels two and three. But, to be honest, I want more for you than a marriage that lasts. Don't get me wrong. I want that! But I want you to know a marriage of deep and lasting joy. I want you to know the fullness of the sacramental grace which will be given to you. I want you to know the unity spoken of in the Song of Solomon in these simple, yet profound, words of love: "My beloved is mine, and I am his" (2:16).

HOW TO DEVELOP A MARRIAGE WITH COMMUNICATION ON ALL THREE LEVELS

Of course, by now you're probably thinking: "Okay. I get the point and yes, I want that too. But how? How can we achieve that kind of deep marital unity?" In answer to your question, to be honest, I don't know. For you see, I don't know you. And since the two of you are unique persons with a unique God-given relationship, there is a very real sense in which only you can answer the question. Just as there are no magic formulas which will guarantee us a deep and lasting relationship with God, so too there are no magic formulas for our marriage relationship. There certainly are many guidelines and many suggestions to get you started. But in each case it will only and can only happen as you work together to make it happen. Get the goal in front of you. Say to yourselves and to each other: "That's what I want and I'm willing to work to make it a reality. I will not be satisfied with a marriage without communication on all three levels."

However, so that you don't despair, let me offer you a few guidelines to get you started.

Firstly, and most importantly, don't look for quick solutions. Build right—build a strong foundation—build for a lifetime. Don't accept short-cuts to marital unity.

FOR
FURTHER
READING:

Five Secrets of a Happy Marriage
by Fr. Gordon and Mary Sue Walker
(Supplement I)

Secondly, get married! Now this may seem like an obvious point, but I believe it is important to stress. At your marriage, when you are brought together by Christ, you will be unified. It is mystical, but the fact is that you leave the wedding different persons with a different relationship. In that ceremony you will be united to each other! That union is real. You see, as a married couple, it is not that you have to create unity, you simply have to live in the unity which is already yours.

Once again, a reference to our spiritual lives helps to explain this point. Prayer does not begin the spiritual life, and prayer does not create our unity with God. Our spiritual life began and was given to us at baptism and chrismation. Prayer develops and is based upon the reality given to us in the sacraments. In the same way, your life together is given to you as a precious gift of God. You don't have to create it; rather, you receive it and develop it. Which means then that the ingredients necessary for developing and maintaining your unity together are not exotic or unusual, but rather are the "common" Christian virtues. Your relationship with each other will be developed and enhanced as you love each other, forgive each other, spend time with each other, and love Christ together.

This last consideration is by far the most important. The unity you will share after your marriage is a unity given you in and through Christ. As Father Stanley Harakas has stated: "The key words in the Orthodox Christian Marriage service are those uttered by the priest as he joins the hands of the couple: he prays to God saying . . . 'and extend Your Hand from Your holy dwelling place and join this Your servant (groom's name) unto this Your servant (bride's name), for by You are husband and wife united . . .' The hands of the bride, the groom, and the priest are joined momentarily at that point in the service, signifying that the couple becomes one in the presence of the Church and through the sanctifying action and grace of God" *(Guidelines for Marriage in the Orthodox Church,* p. 3).

You see, if you are really serious about "real communication" in your marriage, it begins with "real communication" with God. Prayer is more than an illustration of communication in marriage; prayer is its life source. As Saint Theophan the Recluse (nineteenth century) wrote: "The root of life is a free and conscious relationship with God, which then directs everything."

I find Father Anthony Coniaris' explanation to be most helpful and meaningful:

"What we do on the first day of our marriage before the holy altar, we should continue to do throughout life. Just as we invited Christ to bless our marriage that first day, so we should invite Him every day through prayer to be the Third Partner in our marriage. No day should go by without the prayerful renewal of our marriage vows in the presence of God and the invitation to Christ to bless our marriage for that day.

"The daily presence of Christ can make a difference in our marriage. Remember how the wine supply was exhausted at the marriage in Cana. It always does at every wedding. One sees couples enamored of each other who in six months are quarreling. The wine turns to water. But Christ can turn the water of an insipid marriage into the tasteful wine of a joyous union. And how blessed is a marriage where the water has become wine, only those know who have tasted it! So, make it a practice to invite Christ into your marriage each day through prayer. Where He is present there

---

"The joint prayer of husband and wife is a great force. That may be one of the reasons why the enemy is trying to get both of you to break this excellent habit."
— Starets Macarius of Optina

FOR FURTHER READING:

The Family Altar by Deacon Michael Hyatt (Supplement J)

Page 79

will be forgiveness, love, understanding and joy. The closer two people live to the source of love, the greater will be the love that will exist between them. And who is the source of all true love but God? . . .

"Draw close to Christ each day through prayer, participation in the Divine Liturgy, Holy Communion, and the reading of His word and you will discover a closeness to your spouse you never thought possible" (*Getting Ready for Marriage in the Orthodox Church,* pp. 8-9).

According to one study conducted by a famous Harvard professor, one out of two and a half marriages ends in divorce. Yet, only one out of eleven hundred marriages ends in divorce when the couple is united spiritually and expresses that unity through mutual worship and prayer. As one couple commented: "We have found through the years that when two people are near to God, it is difficult for them to get away from each other" (quoted in *Getting Ready for Marriage,* p. 17).

LEARNING TO REALLY LISTEN

Let's go back for a moment to the example of Joyce and Richard I mentioned at the beginning of this chapter. As you remember, Joyce complained to her husband, Richard, that they hadn't really communicated in years. Richard was astonished, and asked, "What do you mean? We talk all the time." Joyce responded, "No, you talk all the time. I just listen."

Obviously, communication is more than just talking. Communication is a process of expressing yourself so that another person understands what you are saying, *and* listening, so that you understand what another person is saying to you.

Listening is perhaps one half of communication. Paul Tournier has said, "It is impossible to overemphasize the immense need humans have to be really listened to. Listen to all the conversations of our world, between nations as well as those between couples. They are, for the most part, dialogues of the deaf" (*To Understand Each Other,* p. 29). Listening—really hearing the other person—is a skill that needs to be developed in marriage.

Keep in mind that listening is a skill that involves more than just use of the ears. Besides hearing the words being spoken, listening involves recognizing the tone of voice used and the many other nonverbal forms of expression.

Think of the simple phrase, "Yes, dear." These two words—depending on tone of voice and accompanying body postures, facial expressions, and actions—can communicate quite different messages. Imagine these words being spoken in a flat tone of voice by a distracted husband, who continues working intently on a project without ever glancing up at his wife. Or imagine these words being spoken in a sarcastic tone of voice by a wife who, with hands on hips, does not agree in the least with what her husband has just said. Obviously, more is being communicated than can be discerned from the spoken words alone.

Sometimes tone of voice and nonverbal expressions are used in a purposeful manner, and shout out a crystal-clear message. At other times, tone of voice and nonverbal forms of communication are subtle, and go unrecognized by one or other of the persons trying to communicate. Some forms of nonverbal communication send different messages to different people, based on cultural or family background. It will be important in your marriage to learn to read each other's body language and facial expressions so that you don't miscommunicate or come to unintentional misunderstandings.

Think about the following meditation by

> "Therefore, my beloved brethren, let every man be swift to hear, slow to speak, slow to wrath."
> —James 1:19

Dr. Kallelis:

Please listen when I talk, but don't only listen with your ears, because if you do, you might not hear what I'm saying, for I do not only talk with my mouth.

Listen with your eyes. Look at me; watch me. My actions may be saying more than my words. You must listen with your eyes because I speak with my eyes. My eyes are the mouthpiece of my inner self, and the inner me is the real me, the me I need you to know.

Listen with your mouth. I need to know that you are hearing me, that you are interested, that you care.

Most of all, listen with your heart, for I talk mainly with my heart. My voice might say, 'How are you, what are you doing?' and your ears may hear this. But my heart might be yelling, 'Ask me how I am; get me to talk; I need to talk!'

If you don't listen with all your heart, you won't hear this, and I will be afraid to really talk to you. But if you listen with your heart, you will hear this, and I will talk and you will listen, and the rainbow will seem to have more color. (*Holy Matrimony,* p. 22.)

To help you think through the important issues presented in this chapter, please work through the following exercises.

1. Summarize your own understanding of effective communication. On the basis of what was presented in this chapter as well as your own reflections, what is the goal you should set for communication in your marriage?

_____

_____

_____

_____

_____

_____

_____

2. In light of your own understanding of communication and the goal
   which you have set for your marriage, analyze both the quality and
   the quantity of the communication in your relationship at each of
   the following three levels.

   a. LEVEL ONE: Sharing ideas, facts, information, opinions, etc.,
      with the other person:

   quantity:_____

   _____

   quality:_____

   _____

   _____

   b. LEVEL TWO: Sharing feelings, desires, longings, hurts, pain,
      etc., with the other person:

   quantity:_____

   _____

   quality:_____

   _____

   _____

   c. LEVEL THREE: Sharing persons—listening, understanding,
      feeling with the other person:

   quantity:_____

   _____

quality:_____

_____

_____

3. As you think about your communication, what areas would you like to see improved? What are your communication strengths and what are your communication weaknesses?

_____

_____

_____

4. What hinders deep communication in your relationship?

   a. You:

   _____

   _____

   _____

   _____

   _____

   b. Your partner:

   _____

   _____

   _____

   _____

   _____

5. Now that you have thought through these issues alone, talk about them with your partner. Compare and contrast your individual answers to questions 1 through 4.

   a. On the basis of your discussions, what are the most important aspects of your OWN communication?

   _____

   _____

_____

_____

_____

_____

b. On the basis of your knowledge of each other and your relationship, isolate the key factors to developing deep unity and communication. How are you going to develop deep and abiding communication in your marriage?

_____

_____

_____

_____

_____

6. Describe your own relationship with God. How can you develop and strengthen this relationship in preparation for your being united to each other in the sacrament of marriage?

_____

_____

_____

_____

7. What kind of listening characterizes your relationship?

_____

_____

_____

_____

_____

8. How successfully do you communicate with your partner on a nonverbal level?

_____

_____

_____

_____

_____

_____

Notes and comments/ things to discuss:

⧢⧣

6

PARTNERS AND HELPERS

"I'm in charge here! I'm the boss."

"Well, I don't care what you call yourself. You can't tell me what to do. I'm my own boss."

As I sit here at my desk beginning this chapter, the fighting words of my children float in through my open window. I'm not alarmed. I know my wife is nearby and the situation will soon be remedied by her calm presence and discerning spirit. But I am reminded of similar discussions I've heard which have alarmed me—discussions not between my two young sons, but between two grown, married adults who have come to my office for counseling.

WHO'S THE BOSS?

Who is in charge? Who is the boss? Who makes the decisions? Who gets the last call?

Disagreement on the answer to these questions is often at the root of marital discord. Therefore, as you continue to work together towards full sacramental union in Christ as a married couple, it is important for you to talk openly and honestly about marital roles and your relationship as husband and wife. My job in this chapter is to help lay the groundwork for that discussion.

From an Orthodox perspective, it is important to begin by asserting that one root problem in

> "In our living together we are one another's hands, ears, and feet. Marriage redoubles our strength, rejoices our friends, causes grief to our enemies. A common concern makes trials bearable."
> —St. Gregory the Theologian

most discussions of marital roles is that the question of authority is equated with that of control. Look back at the questions I listed. Who is in charge? Who makes the decisions? Who is the boss? Notice that the presupposition underlying these questions is that the person in charge is in "control" of the other person. The real question being asked is: "Who gets to dominate the other person? Who is the big cheese? Who calls the shots?"

Orthodoxy has a great difficulty answering these questions because her view of authority is so radically different. In fact, from an Orthodox perspective, the couple who tries to structure their marriage by answering these questions is doomed to failure from the start, regardless of who ends up being in "control." This is because Orthodoxy is fundamentally committed to the concept of "personal freedom."

Take God's authority over man as the prime example. No Orthodox Christian would deny that God is ultimately in charge! Orthodoxy believes in the transcendence of God and the supreme authority He exercises as our Creator and Redeemer. But, unlike some other expressions of Christianity, Orthodoxy does not believe that God's authority does away with man's freedom. This heresy, known as predestination, has always been rejected by the Church as alien and foreign to the message of the Bible.

Man is free. God's sovereignty does not do away with man's freedom but rather affirms it. As Vladimir Lossky comments: "To be in the image of God, the Fathers affirm, in the last analysis is to be a personal being, that is to say, a free responsible being" (*Orthodox Theology*, p. 71). So therefore, God's sovereignty does not deny man's freedom. In fact, "God becomes *powerless* before human freedom" (ibid., p. 73). This explains the common patristic motif of God "as a beggar of love waiting at the soul's door without ever daring to force it" (ibid.). As Saint Gregory of Nyssa correctly summarizes: "God has honored man by granting him freedom."

In a biblical context, to assert God's sovereignty or His "being in charge" is to assert His prime role as initiator, as lover, as suitor. Since God is sovereign, He took the initiative in establishing a relationship with man. He took upon Himself the responsibility to create man and to come to man with a desire for friendship. When man freely chose to turn from Him, God assumed the responsibility to bring man back to Him. He graciously called Abram out of Ur of the Chaldees. He graciously led Moses and the Israelites out of Egypt and brought them to the Promised Land. In the fullness of time, He became man and assumed our fallen humanity so that we might be reunited with deity. In each case God is the great initiator, who acts to establish and then restore man's friendship with Him. But never does God's initiation suppress man's freedom. Rather, it explodes man's freedom, opens up for him new possibilities and new vistas, fills him and helps him be all that he was created to be.

Two crucial points are underscored by this brief theological summary. Firstly, true leadership brings with it the responsibility to initiate and to restore. Secondly, true leadership never seeks to control but always to set free. Authority is not to be equated with control. Authority is rather to be equated with initiatory love and sacrifice.

When marital roles are discussed, the Orthodox question is not "Who is in charge?" but rather, "Who is primarily responsible before God to initiate and to restore?" In an Orthodox marriage, no one should feel controlled or dominated. Freedom must be the hallmark of each marriage. "Where the Spirit of the Lord is, there is freedom." A fundamental requirement for loving marriage

> "Do you want to have your wife obedient to you, as the Church is to Christ? Then take yourself the same provident care for her as Christ takes for the Church. Yes, even if it becomes necessary for you to give your life for her, yes, and to be cut into pieces ten thousand times, yes, and to endure and undergo any suffering whatever, do not refuse it."
> —St. John Chrysostom

is that each person is freely choosing the relationship. This is why the wedding service begins with the question: "Is this a free choice you have made?" Marriage does not enslave; rather, it sets free!

Thus we see that marital roles and the relationship of husband and wife are totally transformed by the realities of the Christian gospel. Outside of Christ and His liberating love, the marriage relationship degenerates into an issue of control and domination. However, in Christ, marriage becomes a context in which each partner is set free by the affirming love of the other—free to be the person God calls him or her to be, free to grow and develop from the inside out rather than the outside in, free to love and to respond to love, free to submit, free to lead.

Only when these thoughts are taken into consideration does Saint Paul's directive concerning marriage make sense:

> Wives, submit to your own husbands, as to the Lord. For the husband is head of the wife, as also Christ is head of the church; and He is the Savior of the body. Therefore, just as the church is subject to Christ, so let the wives be to their own husbands in everything. Husbands, love your wives, just as Christ also loved the church and gave Himself for her, that He might sanctify and cleanse her with the washing of water by the word, that He might present her to Himself a glorious church, not having spot or wrinkle or any such thing, but that she should be holy and without blemish. So husbands ought to love their own wives as their own bodies; he who loves his wife loves himself. For no one ever hated his own flesh, but nourishes and cherishes it, just as the Lord

does the church (Ephesians 5:22-29).

THE REAL DIFFERENCES BETWEEN MEN AND WOMEN

There is a difference, a God-created difference, between men and women. This is a fundamental tenet of biblical anthropology. Humanity, as originally created by God, is comprised of two different, complementary sexes. "Male and female He created them," the Book of Genesis recounts. Orthodoxy believes that there is a constitutional (ontological) difference between men and women. Therefore, any attempt to unsex humanity is an attempt to dehumanize humanity. As anthropologist Margaret Mead has argued: "Every adjustment that minimizes a difference, a vulnerability, in one sex, a differential strength in the other, diminishes the possibility of complementing each other, and leads to a duller vision of human life in which is denied the fullness of humanity that each might have had" (*Male and Female,* pp. 32-33).

What is this God-created difference? Paul Evdokimov answers: "The nature of man is to act; that of woman is to be" (*The Sacrament of Love,* p. 39). Man interacts with his environment through extension; woman through internalization. To use the words we have already discussed, man by nature initiates, woman responds. These are not sexist comments—just basic biblical insights into the nature of humanity as created by God.

Therefore, as Saint Paul outlines the order of marriage, he appeals to men to pattern their initiation, their activity, after Christ's, and he appeals to women to pattern their response after the Church's. It is not a legal question of authority which is being discussed. Marriage, as the sacrament of love, transcends and explodes legal restrictions. Rather, Saint Paul here describes the re-establishment of our united humanity in Christ in the sacrament of marriage.

FOR FURTHER READING:
Does Equal Mean the Same? by Fr. John Weldon Hardenbrook (Supplement K)
Imago Dei by Fr. Thomas Hopko (Supplement L)

Page 91

Something perverse happened at the Fall. The harmonious relationship of initiation and response between man and woman under God was destroyed. Man saw himself as controller and woman as the controlled. His masculinity became increasingly defined by ownership, by claiming something for himself, by restriction rather than emancipation. Woman, on the other hand, was no longer fulfilled by responding to the leadership of another. She took it upon herself to initiate, to develop, to claim independence for herself and to reject the leadership of the male. The war of the sexes began in earnest.

In Christ the war of the sexes has come to an end. Man and woman in marriage complement each other. The husband is called to give—to spend and be spent for his wife. It is his responsibility to initiate, to look out for his wife, to love her, to cherish her, to guard her in her areas of weakness and to support her in her strengths. When problems arise and the relationship deteriorates, it is his responsibility to sacrifice—his pride, his money, his life if need be—to bring restoration. The wife is called to respond—to receive his love and to reciprocate in kind. She is to find her strength in his, to wait upon him to lead, to build him up, to encourage him to grow and develop, to support him and stand by him even in his failures.

This distinction between initiation and response should not be thought of as a distinction between active and passive behavior. Once again, we return to Orthodox theology to help us think clearly. In the accomplishment of our salvation, God initiates and we respond. Our response, however, is more than passive acceptance of God's will. Orthodoxy requires of us active participation in the will and action of God. We call this the doctrine of "synergy." We work together with God to accomplish our salvation. We cooperate with Him; we work out our salvation, for it is God who works in us. Our submission to God does not deny our activity; rather, it channels it appropriately.

Likewise, in marriage the husband and wife must work together; they must cooperate with each other in order to experience the full grace of their sacramental union. Yes, the husband must lead and the wife must submit to his leadership. But this combination of leadership and submission, initiation and response, is not that of superior to inferior; nor is it that of active agent to passive. Rather, it is a relationship of cooperation, of synergy.

In being called to submit, the wife is not called to be a doormat, passively accepting whatever her husband throws her way. She is not called to deny her own God-given abilities, remaining "barefoot, pregnant, and in the kitchen." Such concepts are a total perversion of the Christian understanding of marriage. However, in being called to submit, the wife is called to use all of her God-given talents and abilities in accordance with her husband's desires and will.

Submission is a matter of the will. When we submit to God, we say, "Thy will be done." We willingly accept His will as our own, and we channel all of our gifts, abilities, and talents to the fulfillment, not of our selfish desires, but of His desires for us. Likewise, in marriage the wife is called to accept her husband's leadership.

The husband is the pacesetter, the visionary, the one who charts the course. Now, undoubtedly, in his chart-setting he must look to his wife for input and inquire as to her desires. This is how Christ leads us. He listens to us and charts a path for us which is in keeping with who we are.

This means that the husband must never function independently of his wife. Remember the motif of God as a beggar of love, waiting at the door, but not forcing it—this is a perfect picture of the husband's leadership. He should never force his wife, but must woo her and plead

> "Nothing is more powerful than a pious and sensible woman to bring her husband into proper order, and to mold his soul as she wills.
> For he will not listen to friends, or teachers, or rulers, as much as he will his partner advising and counseling him, since the advice carries some pleasures with it, because she who gives the counsel is greatly loved."
> — St. John Chrysostom

with her and stand at the door of her heart as a "beggar of love," persistently knocking but never forcing his way in.

A wonderful picture of this is given in Proverbs 31. The woman described is multi-talented and is very active in the exercise of her gifts. "She seeks wool and flax, and willingly works with her hands. She is like the merchant ships, she brings her food from afar. . . . She considers a field and buys it; from her profits she plants a vineyard. She girds herself with strength, and strengthens her arms. . . . She makes linen garments and sells them, and supplies sashes for the merchants. . . . She opens her mouth with wisdom, and on her tongue is the law of kindness" (vv. 13-26). No doubt here is a woman who has been set free by her husband to be the person God has created her to be. She is not some passive, doormat figure, waiting at home for her husband's direction on every issue. She is creative; she develops and plans and implements. But she is not independent. For the text says: "The heart of her husband safely trusts her. . . . She does him good and not evil all the days of her life" (vv. 11, 12).

Sadly, this beautiful picture is often perverted by human sin. Some women fight their husbands and refuse to submit to their leadership. Some men fight their wives and refuse to allow them freedom. Worse still, some husbands refuse to lead and, in the absence of male leadership, force their wives to function independently. In each case, the marriage suffers, and the deep union created by working together with each other is not achieved.

NOTE: As you think through your answers to the questions in this section, be prepared to discuss the issues raised at your next session with your priest. Be aware of the fact that this is an incredibly emotional subject. Don't attack your partner, but attempt to share with him/her your true feelings. Also, don't let fear of controversy or disagreement keep you from talking about these issues. For your marriage to be what God intends it to be, you must be free enough to discuss your feelings—both positive and negative—with your partner. If your fear is so great that you cannot discuss it with your partner, this may indicate some serious problems in your relationship which must be resolved. If this is the case, schedule a private appointment with your priest to talk about it.

To help you think through the issues raised in this chapter, answer the following questions:

1. As you think about your relationship, are there any ways and/or areas in which you have felt trapped or controlled by your partner?

_____

_____

_____

_____

2. Do you feel that your partner is setting you free to be the person God has called you to be, or trying to force you into a mold he/she has created for you? Does freedom characterize your relationship?

_____

_____

_____

_____

3. One of the difficult areas which often arises when couples discuss freedom is the notion of "personal time" versus "time together." Jot down your response to these questions. If you can, talk about this with your partner. However, if you think it is too emotional, wait until you meet with your priest.

a. How much time alone do you need?

_____

_____

_____

_____

b. Have there been disagreements over this issue?

_____

_____

_____

c. Does one partner feel smothered by the other?

_____

_____

_____

d. Does one partner feel jealous about the other person's use of time?

_____

_____

_____

4. Many times conflicts arise in marriage because there has been no clear discussion of goals. Each partner brings his or her own goals to the marriage and pursues these goals independently. For you to be partners and helpers, it is important that you work through and develop goals both of you can work on together. Obviously, in light of the teaching of this chapter, it is the husband's responsibility to take the leadership, but he must listen carefully to his wife and, together, they must arrive at mutually shared goals.

Talk about your personal and joint goals for your lives and marriage. Make sure you discuss the following areas:

- family life (size of family, time spent with extended family, vacations, etc.)
- money management (budget, spending habits, saving accounts, etc.)
- spiritual life (church attendance, family prayer time, personal daily prayer rules, etc.)
- friendships and relationships with others (who, how often, etc.)
- careers and occupational goals (desired yearly income, whether both partners will work, etc.)

If there are areas where you cannot agree, please talk about them with your priest during the next session. Record any areas where you need further discussion to arrive at a mutually shared goal.

_____

_____

_____

_____

_____

_____

5. As a springboard for your discussions regarding family spirituality, read together "The Family Altar" (Supplement J, at the back of the book). Use this article to help focus your own thoughts, beliefs, and feelings in this area, and map out a plan for your spiritual life as a family.

_____

_____

_____

_____

_____

_____

_____

_____

6. Conflicts also can arise because there has been no clear delineation of responsibilities. Look over the following list of responsibilities and discuss who will be *primarily* "in charge." On the blank space next to each descriptive phrase, indicate who will be mainly responsible for the area described.

_____ a. Money management (establishing budget)

_____ b. Finances and bookkeeping (paying bills, keeping records)

_____ c. Purchasing food and household goods

_____ d. Menu planning and cooking

_____ e. Housecleaning

_____ f. Spiritual oversight (church selection, attendance, morning and evening prayers)

_____ g. Family activities (fun times, recreation, family projects)

_____ h. Vacation plans

_____ i. Clothing purchasing

_____ j. Transportation (automobile selection and maintenance)

_____ k. Hospitality

_____ l. Gift planning and purchase

_____ m. Memorabilia keeping (family records, pictures, newspaper clippings, letters)

_____ n. Special events (birthdays, anniversaries)

_____ o. Furniture (selection, purchases, and maintenance)

_____ p. Time and schedule organizing

_____ q. Yardwork and gardening

_____ r. Family health services

_____ s. Correspondence (family letters, keeping up with friends)

List other responsibilities that will be the primary responsibility of one spouse:

_____ / _____

_____ / _____

_____ / _____

_____ / _____

7. Read Proverbs 31, then write a brief description of what you believe would be an ideal, modern-day "Proverbs 31" wife and mother. Also describe her modern-day counterpart—the ideal husband and father.

a. My ideal of an excellent wife and mother:

_____

_____

_____

_____

b. My ideal of an excellent husband and father:

_____

_____

_____

_____

c. Compare your ideals for an excellent wife/husband with your partner's ideals. In what ways are they similar/different? How closely do you meet your partner's ideals? How closely do you meet your own ideals?

_____

_____

_____

_____

Notes and comments/things to discuss:

7

MONEY MANAGEMENT

MONEY! What thoughts come into your head as you read this word? It is amazing how many different reactions one simple word can bring. Many are obsessed with the word, spending most of their time trying to figure out ways to get more. Others are afraid of it, seeing it as a source (if not *the* source) of all that is wrong with our world. Still others don't quite know what to make of it, convinced that "you can't live with it, and you can't live without it."

In almost every marriage, at some point there is conflict over money and its proper management. Should we buy a new car? How big a house should we buy and how big a loan should we take? Should we buy things on credit? If we do, how much debt load can we carry? Should we save this money or should we give it away? Do we really need a bigger television set? How much should we spend on Christmas gifts? The list of possible questions and possible conflicts is endless.

What is a proper Orthodox world-view regarding money and finances? How do God and the Church figure in the picture? How can you as a couple take control of your finances, rather than letting your finances take control of you? These are some of the questions that need to be answered in this chapter.

> "He who holds possessions as the gifts of God . . . and knows that what he possesses is for the sake of others is blessed by God and poor in spirit."
> — St. Clement of Alexandria

"Ponder the truth of Christian marriage: man and wife are one flesh! Does it not follow that they must share all their possessions? And yet you two haggle over this property! And why? Because of words! Unless you promptly strive for and achieve a loving peace between you, it is hopeless to try to bring tidiness and fairness into your business dealings with one another."

—Starets Macarius

Very often, disagreements over money matters stem from different understandings of the purpose of money. Basically, people tend to think of money in two different ways. Some believe that money is for security. Money is to be used carefully, for necessary items, and the rest is to be saved "for a rainy day." Others believe money is for pleasure and enjoyment. Some money may be saved for emergencies, but beyond that the rest is to be spent so that we may enjoy ourselves.

These different approaches can create conflict. Take Tom and Elizabeth, for example. Tom is one who sees money as pleasure and Elizabeth sees money as security. When Tom has a few extra dollars in his pocket, he stops and buys his wife something. Most of the time he picks up something she doesn't need but might enjoy—flowers, jewelry, etc. Each time when he comes home and surprises her with these gifts, he senses that she is not really excited about what he has done. Usually she asks him where he got the money to buy them. In the beginning Tom is confused. As it continues he becomes bitter and resentful: "Doesn't she love me? Doesn't she want my love? Does she want to control me? Whose money is it, anyway? Doesn't she trust me to make the right decisions?"

As Tom struggles with these thoughts and feelings, his wife is struggling with others. Since she believes that money is for security, she doesn't understand why he keeps wasting money on things which she doesn't need. "Doesn't he know that we are going to need a new car soon? Can't he see that the children's shoes are wearing out? How does he expect us to pay for these things if he is wasting money on these silly things?" Her fear grows, as does her lack of trust in Tom's ability to provide for the family. She begins to nag him about how he spends money.

Of course, you can easily see how the scenario

will continue to disintegrate. The sad thing is that it is not necessary. Both Tom and Elizabeth are operating quite consistently with their own understanding. Each one is trying to show love. Tom is trying to show love by spending money on bringing pleasure to his wife instead of himself. Before he was married he would spend those few dollars for a burger and fries. Now he buys flowers. Elizabeth is trying to show love by providing for the well-being and future prosperity of the family. She doesn't want the money for herself. She wants it for her children. But neither of them is able to see the other's love. He thinks she is a nag and doesn't trust him to provide for the family. She thinks he is careless of the real needs of the family.

How can this be resolved? First, both Tom and Elizabeth need to try to understand each other before they judge. Understanding why the other is acting that particular way helps us not to attribute false motives to them. It helps us appreciate the intent, even if we disagree with the action. Second, both Tom and Elizabeth need to submit their own understanding of money to a larger vision for money which can fuse both perspectives into one. This is the perspective of the Orthodox Faith: Money is for ministry! God gives us the resources of this world so that we might minister to others.

What does this mean? To assist you in focussing your thoughts and your discussion of money matters, I will be giving you three reading assignments from the supplements in the back of this book. Please read each one carefully and answer the questions which are listed here. There are no easy answers when it comes to the settling of financial questions within marriage. But having a common commitment to the basic principle that what you have is given you by God, not to serve yourselves but to serve others, will help you maintain marital unity even as you work through

"Give them of the dew of heaven from on high, and of the fatness of the earth. Fill their houses with every good thing, so that they may in turn give to those in need.... So that, having sufficiency in all things, they may abound in every good work that is good and acceptable to You."
—Prayers from the Orthodox wedding liturgy

the different ways in which this principle can and must be applied in your lives together.

To apply the first section of this chapter to your lives, first answer questions 1 and 2 individually:

1. Which of the following best characterizes your personal view of money? (If one view does not predominate, rank them in order of importance in your life.)

    _____ Money is security. (Use it carefully, for necessary items, and save the rest "for a rainy day.")

    _____ Money is for pleasure and enjoyment. (Save some money for emergencies, but spend the rest to enjoy yourself.)

    _____ Money is for ministry. (God gives us the resources of this world so that we might minister to others.)

2. Which of the following do you think best characterizes your partner's personal view of money? (If one view does not predominate, rank them in order of importance in his/her life.)

    _____ Money is security.

    _____ Money is for pleasure and enjoyment.

    _____ Money is for ministry.

3. Now spend some time as a couple discussing your basic views and orientation regarding money.

    Are your views the same?

    _____

    Did you characterize your partner's views in the same way he/she characterized his/her own views?

    _____

    How will you work to resolve conflicts regarding money management arising from different views of money?

    _____
    _____
    _____

ASSIGNMENT #1: READ Supplement M ("On Tithing," beginning on page 197).

1. Answer questions 1a through 1e individually:
   a. How did the family you grew up in approach the subject of tithing and charitable giving?

   _____

   _____

   _____

   b. In the church in which you are a member, is tithing or pledging the common or expected practice?

   _____

   c. Do you personally agree with the principle of tithing and the four guidelines mentioned in the article?

   _____

   _____

   d. Do you currently tithe? Do you currently pledge? How much do you currently give to the church in an average month?

   _____

   _____

   e. What are your goals for charitable giving?

   _____

   _____

2. Spend some time as a couple discussing and coming to an agreement on how you will deal with tithing, pledging, and almsgiving in your marriage. Our charitable giving goals are:

   _____

   _____

   _____

   _____

ASSIGNMENT #2: READ Supplement N ("The Battle for the Billfold," beginning on page 202).

1. Answer questions 1a and 1b individually:
   a. What are your personal goals and expectations with regard to money and possessions? Do you presently live by the NBMM Syndrome? Is it your goal to become "sharing-oriented" rather than "consumer-oriented"?

   _____

   _____

   _____

   _____

   _____

   _____

   b. List some of the general purchasing principles your family lived by when you were growing up.

   _____

   _____

   _____

   _____

   _____

2. Compare your personal goals and expectations with your partner's. Are they compatible? Are they realistic for you as a couple?

   _____

   _____

   _____

   _____

   _____

3. Compare the general purchasing principles each of you grew up with. What general purchasing principles do you want to establish for your own marriage?

   _____

_____

_____

_____

_____

4. Discuss your attitudes and goals regarding the purchase of the
   following items:

   a. Automobiles _____

   _____

   b. Major appliances _____

   _____

   c. Furniture and household items _____

   _____

   d. Clothing _____

   _____

   e. Groceries _____

   _____

5. What priority do you place on the four items listed in the article as
   being important for a financial game plan:

   a. Cash savings _____

   b. Insurance coverage _____

   c. Investments _____

   d. Drawing up a will _____

6. Are your views on these subjects the same? In what ways?

   _____

_____

_____

_____

7. Define a financial game plan that you can both live by:

_____

_____

_____

_____

_____

_____

_____

ASSIGNMENT #3: READ Supplement O ("Spending Wisely," beginning on page 207).

Questions for Engaged Couples:
1. What are your financial priorities?

_____

_____

_____

2. Has either of you prepared and lived according to a budget in the past? If so, did you have the self-discipline necessary to follow through with it?

_____

_____

3. Besides food and shelter, what are some of the things you "can't live without"?

_____

_____

_____

4. Does either of you have a savings account? Does either of you have any outstanding debts your partner needs to be aware of? In the past, has either of you had difficulty living within your means?

_____

_____

_____

5. Take time now to draw up a preliminary budget. (Complete the process in greater detail before your marriage.)

a. Start by each of you determining accurately your current actual expenses and income for a typical month.

Category	Bride-to-be	Husband-to-be
Monthly income	_____	_____
Charitable giving	_____	_____
Rent	_____	_____
Utilities	_____	_____
Food	_____	_____
Transportation	_____	_____
Clothing	_____	_____
Insurance	_____	_____
Entertainment	_____	_____
Other :	_____	_____
_____	_____	_____
_____	_____	_____
_____	_____	_____
_____	_____	_____

b. Then determine the joint income you anticipate after you are married, and estimate as closely as possible your typical joint monthly expenses.

Category	Estimated amounts after marriage
Monthly income	_____
Charitable giving	_____
Rent	_____
Utilities	_____
Food	_____

Transportation   _____

Clothing   _____

Insurance   _____

Entertainment   _____

Other :   _____

_____   _____

_____   _____

_____   _____

_____   _____

_____   _____

_____   _____

c. How will you handle all the one-time extraordinary expenses involved in setting up housekeeping during the first year? Make a list of potential expenses (including wedding expenses which will not be paid for prior to your wedding.)

d. What life-style changes will you need to make for you to "balance the budget"?

e. Who will be primarily responsible for bill-paying and record-keeping? _____

f. How will you coordinate your spending?

g. How will you deal with the situation if one or the other of you has overspent?

_____

_____

_____

h. How will you decide to make necessary adjustments to the budget you have set up?

_____

_____

_____

Questions for those who are already married:

1. What are your financial priorities?

_____

_____

_____

2. Have you as a couple ever prepared and lived according to a budget? If so, did you have any difficulties following through with it?

_____

_____

_____

3. Are there some things one of you feels you "can't live without" that the other feels are frivolous or not necessary?

_____

_____

_____

4. Do you have a savings account? What are your savings goals? Do you have outstanding debts? Do you have a plan for retiring these debts? Have you as a couple had difficulty living within your means?

_____

_____

_____

_____

5. a. What are your current actual expenses and income for a typical
    month?

Category	Current Amount
Monthly income	_____
Charitable giving	_____
Rent	_____
Utilities	_____
Food	_____
Transportation	_____
Clothing	_____
Insurance	_____
Entertainment	_____
Other :	_____
_____	_____
_____	_____
_____	_____
_____	_____
_____	_____
_____	_____

b. What life-style changes do you need to make for you to "balance
   the budget"?

_____

_____

c. Who is currently responsible for bill-paying and record-keeping?

   _____

   Are you both comfortable with how this works out on a day-to-
   day basis? If not, what changes would you like to make?

_____

_____

d. How do you currently coordinate your spending? Have any

problems occurred in this area? If so, how can you better coordinate your spending in the future?

_____

_____

_____

_____

_____

_____

e. How have you dealt with the situation when one or the other of you has overspent? If this caused friction in your marriage, how can you establish a way of dealing with these types of problems?

_____

_____

_____

_____

f. How do you decide if and when it is time to make adjustments to your spending habits? If this has caused problems in your marriage, set up some guidelines for dealing with this in the future.

_____

_____

_____

g. If you don't currently live by a budget, do you believe that the discipline of maintaining a budget would help you manage your money and reduce conflict in your marriage? _____

If so, are you both willing and committed to come up with a workable budget and live by it for a year (or some other specified period of time)? _____

Notes and comments/things to discuss:

8

SEXUALITY IN MARRIAGE

Modern Christians live in a world which places incredible importance upon sex in relationships. Our lustful American culture seems to believe that a marital relationship—or almost any intimate human relationship—will only be as good as the sex within the relationship. "To have a good relationship it is necessary to have good sex," they say. Hence, the development of sex therapists and the abundant printing of how-to-have-good-sex books and videos. It is truly believed that without "good sex," a relationship is doomed.

Sadly, the modern "Christian" world seems to believe this message as well. It has "Christianized" the rhetoric a bit and toned down the bizarre side of modern sexuality by creating "Christian" alternatives to secular sex therapists and secular sexual help books, but it has bought the same basic bottom line.

The impact of this on marriages has been enormous. Sadly, it is now common for Christian couples to divorce each other over "sexual incompatibility." "She's not good in bed" has become, even to many who would consider themselves serious Christians, a legitimate reason for questioning the viability of a marriage. Sexual performance has become a great concern. Achieving sexual orgasm is high on the list of marital objectives.

> "Let marriage be held in honor among all, and let the marriage bed be undefiled."
> —Hebrews 13:4

The soundness of people's marriages is rated by the frequency of their sexual intercourse.

How should we as Orthodox men and women look upon the subject of sexual relations in marriage? To begin with, it is important to state the obvious. Sexual relations within marriage are holy and blessed by God. Saint Gregory the Theologian says: "Are you not yet married in the flesh? Do not fear this consecration; you are pure even after marriage" (*Oration on Holy Baptism,* quoted by George Gabriel, *You Call My Words Immodest,* p. 3). The sexual union of man and woman in Christian marriage is sanctified, set apart, hallowed, sacred, holy. And it is good.

At the same time—and I cannot emphasize this point strongly enough—the Church teaches us clearly that sex is not *the essence* of Christian marriage. Sex, being of this world, is not essential. If in our thinking it ever becomes essential, then we are wrong and we need to repent of our ungodly way of thinking (see Romans 12:2).

As we shall see, in the majority of marriages, sexual relations have a vital role to play in the maintenance and expression of that union in this world, but its role is limited to this world. Many of the Fathers teach that there were no sexual relations in paradise before the Fall. Although "good," sexual relations are destined to "pass away." There will be no sexual relations after the Resurrection (see Matthew 22:23-32), but the union of man and woman in Christian marriage endures forever. It has to, because true Christian love "never fails" (1 Corinthians 13:8).

FINDING THE BALANCE

From the beginning, the Church has sought to establish this godly balance in the lives of married believers. This is why she expects members to fast from sex in marriage—to abstain completely from sexual expression—at various periods in their lives, so that they might devote their attention fully to the Kingdom which is not of this world. Orthodox Christians are called upon to fast from sexual relations whenever preparing to receive Holy Communion. Likewise, we abstain on the eve of all major feast days and Sundays, and at various times throughout the year according to the Church calendar. Ask your priest for guidelines regarding specific dates and periods.

Some Orthodox saints have even been called upon to abstain completely from that which is good in marriage itself. The holy martyrs Cecilia and Valerian gave themselves entirely to God from the very first night of their arranged marriage. They were united in spiritual vision during a time of intense Roman persecution in the early Church. After great struggle for the Faith, they died together as martyrs for the love of Christ.

More recently, Saint John of Kronstadt and his wife lived together in the same manner, so that Saint John could give himself over more completely to the tremendous burden of ministry that God placed upon him as a priest in nineteenth-century Russia.

Throughout her history, the Church has greatly honored these, and a host of other married saints who lived in the same way, as worthy of veneration. They exercise a prophetic role, reminding us all of the exalted nature and purpose of the marital union. But not all are so called.

Many of the saints engaged in marital relations. The great Apostle Peter was married and I know of nothing in our tradition which implies that he ceased having sexual relations with his wife. Saint Philip had children. Saint Innocent of Alaska lived physically with his wife, becoming monastic only when she died. Saint Terence and his wife, Neonila, had seven children. All nine of them, martyred in the second century in Syria, are canonized saints of the Church.

> "[Marriage] is the harbor of chastity for those who desire to use it well, and it renders one's nature not to be wild. For like a dam, marriage gives us an opportunity for legitimate intercourse and in this way contains the waves of sexual desire. It places us in a great calm and watches over us."
> —St. John Chrysostom

The marital relations of Saints Basil the Elder and Emmelia resulted in the birth of ten children, one of whom died in childhood. Of the remaining nine children, five of them are canonized saints. Two of them, Saint Macrina and Saint Naucratius, were godly monastics. The other three, Peter of Sebaste, Gregory of Nyssa, and Basil the Great, were saintly bishops, the latter two being outstanding Fathers of the Church. These are a few examples of many. But they are sufficient to illustrate the point that godly sexual intercourse was practiced by many of God's holy people.

As Orthodox Christians, we are called to healthy, balanced living in all areas of our lives, including this important area of sexuality. We must not be consumed by the world's compulsive designs—we do not dance to the same drumbeat. Neither are we called to puritanical legalism, embarrassed by the thought of marital sexuality. There is a time and a place in God's universe for all things done in humble submission to His holy calling.

Saint John Chrysostom writes: "If for a certain period, you and your wife have abstained by agreement, perhaps for a time of prayer and fasting, come together again for the sake of your marriage. You do not need procreation as an excuse. It is not the chief reason for marriage. Neither it is necessary to allow for the possibility of conceiving, and thus having a large number of children, something you may not want" (*On Virginity,* quoted by Gabriel, ibid., p. 3). Sexual desire in marriage is not something to be ashamed of. Once again, Saint John states: "Desire is not sin. But when it falls into immoderation and will not remain within the laws of marriage, and spills over to the wives of others, it then becomes adultery, not because of desire but because of insatiability" (*13th Homily on Romans*).

A SPIRITUAL TRANSFIGURATION

In Christian marriage, sex, like so many other aspects of our lives, undergoes a transfiguration. In the world, sex is an expression of lust, of conquest, of using others for the satisfaction of self. This is why, in the moral disintegration of this fallen world, preoccupation with sex inescapably leads to and is linked with preoccupation with violence and death. Unbridled, nonsanctified sexual activity is satanic, filled with the devil's hatred of God, mankind, and life itself. It is suicidal.

In Christian marriage, sex is rescued from Satan's grasp. In His Resurrection, Christ destroyed death by death. He has granted us immortality precisely because "he has destroyed the power of death and the devil, liberating men and women from a sexuality of death. That is, from the sexuality of domination, of power, of reproductive competition; from the sexuality of the herd and the survival of the species, or the tribe; from the sexuality of previously unredeemed humanity" (Gabriel, op. cit., p. 6).

Flowing out of these comments comes a very positive understanding of marital sexuality. The goal of sex in marriage is spiritual union. Through the joining of two physical bodies in marital love comes a unique oneness of soul. Saint John Chrysostom instructs us: "Their intercourse accomplishes the joining of their bodies, and they are made one, just as when perfume is mixed with ointment" *(12th Homily on Colossians).*

The 13th Canon of the Sixth Ecumenical Council, in refuting the requirement of priestly celibacy, ascribes to sex the positive role of strengthening marital unity: "Since we have learned that in the Church of the Romans it is regarded as tantamount to a canon that candidates for ordination to the diaconate or presbyterate must solemnly promise to have no further intercourse with their wives, we, however, continuing in conformity with the ancient canon of Apostolic rigorism and orderliness, desire henceforth that the lawful marriages of ordained men *be made stronger.* And we are in no way dissolving their intercourse with their wives, nor depriving them of *their mutual relationship and companionship"* (emphasis added).

The unity of our persons is such that what we do with our bodies, we do with our souls. We bow the neck of our soul by bowing the neck of our body. Our souls prostrate through the prostration of our bodies. What our bodies do, our souls do. Furthermore, as Christians, both our bodies and our souls belong to Christ. Through baptism they have become His members. Therefore, for a Christian, sexual union is not just physical; it is also spiritual. Saint Paul writes: "Do you not know that your bodies are members of Christ? Shall I then take the members of Christ and make them members of a harlot? Certainly not!" (1 Corinthians 6:15). According to the Apostle, a union that is more than physical takes place in sex.

Following the same argument, since sex is something more than physical, in Christian marriage when you have sex with your spouse, you take the members of Christ (your body) and unite them with the members of Christ (your spouse's body); the two become one in Christ. This sexual union is blessed by God. Its purpose is not primarily physical pleasure, but the spiritual union of your spouse and yourself in Christ.

Please understand, this union is accomplished only when sexual relations take place within Christian marriage in the context of "sanctification and honor" (1 Thessalonians 4:4). It is important to note that sex is not always "good" just because it occurs within the confines of Christian marriage. In marriage, sexual relations which are the fruit of "passionate lust" or are the expression of violence and/or physical control are not blessed. In Christian marriage, sexual relations must always be freely entered into and must never be forced. Manipulation in sexual matters is always inappropriate. Likewise, any sexual union outside of marriage is a union with death. But within Christian marriage, blessed sexual intimacy is life-giving.

PROCREATION AND BIRTH CONTROL

The most obvious example of the life-giving nature of marital sexual intimacy is the conception of children. The marriage service over and over again holds this forth as both a blessing and a goal of Christian marriage: "Give them the fruit of the womb, fair children, concord of soul and body. Exalt them like the cedars of Lebanon, like a luxuriant vine; bestow on them a rich store of substance, so that having a sufficiency of all things for themselves, they may abound in every good work that is good and acceptable before You. Let them see their children's children as newly planted olive trees around their table; so that finding favor before You, they may shine like the stars in the heavens, in You, our God." "Stretch forth Your hand from Your holy dwelling place, and join together this Your servant and this Your handmaid. For by You is a wife joined to her husband. Unite them in oneness of mind; wed them into one flesh; grant them the fruit of the womb and the procreation of fair children." The implication of these prayers is very clear. Sexual intimacy in marriage is very much connected to procreation. Procreation is not the only purpose of sex in marriage, but sex and procreation go hand in hand.

One modern summary of the Church's tradition states:

The greatest miracle and blessing of the divinely sanctified love of marriage is the procreation of children, and to avoid

"Wed them into one flesh; grant them the fruit of the womb and the procreation of fair children."
—a prayer from the Orthodox wedding liturgy

this by the practice of birth control (or, more accurately, the prevention of conception) is against God's will for marriage. . . . In all the difficult decisions involving the practice of birth control, Orthodox families must live under the guidance of the pastors of the Church and ask daily for the mercy and forgiveness of God.

Orthodox husbands and wives must discuss the prevention of conception in the light of the circumstances of their own personal lives, having in mind always the normal relationship between the divinely sanctified love of marriage and the begetting of children. Conception control of any sort motivated by selfishness or lack of trust in God's providential care certainly cannot be condoned (*Documents of the Orthodox Church in America: Marriage*, pp. 17, 18).

Each couple should seek the guidance and counsel of their own spiritual father in making decisions about birth control. This is especially crucial in our day and age, because within the Church there are varying opinions concerning how these standards are to be applied. All would agree adamantly, however, that any birth control method that employs, either as primary or secondary mechanism, something that kills a fertilized egg or prevents it from implanting itself on the uterine wall may not and must not be used, because the Church has universally stood against abortion in any form.

Any couple using or planning to use any form of contraception control should discuss these issues frankly and openly with their spiritual father. Allow him to guide you in this all-important area of your lives together.

UNSELFISH LOVE AND SELF-DENIAL

Having said all of this about procreation, however, we must expand our understanding of the life-giving nature of sexual relations and include not only procreation, but also the development of true companionship between the husband and the wife and the expression of the love of the husband and wife in sacrificial ministry towards each other. Sexual relations provide an opportunity for the development of a spirit of martyrdom. This is the type of martyrdom that exhibits self-denial and submission to the other. Saint Paul puts it this way:

> Let the husband render to his wife the affection due her, and likewise also the wife to her husband. The wife does not have authority over her own body, but the husband does. And likewise the husband does not have authority over his own body, but the wife does (1 Corinthians 7:3, 4).

The call to deny oneself in an act of loving submission to one's spouse is the kind of sacrificial love that transforms us. This laying down of life for the good of the other belongs in our bedroom as much as it does in any other aspect of our life. The promise of God concerning your marriage is that if the two of you together attain unselfish love towards each other and the needy around you and the denial of self, you will suffer a bloodless martyrdom and the mystery of your crowning will be fulfilled.

Through your marriage, may the words of Saint Paul become yours: "For I am already being poured out as a drink offering, and the time of my departure is at hand. I have fought the good fight, I have finished the race, I have kept the faith. Finally, there is laid up for me the crown of righteousness, which the Lord, the righteous Judge, will give to me on that Day, and not to me only

but also to all who have loved His appearing"
(2 Timothy 4:6-8).

QUESTIONS FOR THOUGHT AND DISCUSSION:

In this chapter I have attempted to summarize for you some important issues in the Church's teaching on sex in marriage. I have also suggested to you that this view of sex is radically different from that of our surrounding culture. It is very important that you understand how you have been influenced by your culture and in what areas you need to change your thinking. Beyond a shadow of a doubt, this is one of the most important things you need to do to ensure a God-pleasing marriage. Both you and your spouse need to agree to understand sex in light of the Church's teaching. This is especially true if you are already married.

> **Note for Engaged Couples:**
> If you are preparing for marriage, be very careful as you work your way through these questions. Preserving your sexual purity is absolutely the most important thing you can do in this area. If talking about sexuality arouses desires that are too strong for you to handle, please stop and talk through this chapter when you meet with your priest.

1. In your own words, summarize the Orthodox Church's teaching on sex in marriage.

_____

_____

_____

_____

_____

2. As you were growing up, what was the prevailing attitude of your parents towards sex? Did they talk freely about sex? What did they say? What kind of instruction did they give you? Were they openly affectionate with you? With each other? How does your family's attitude towards sex compare and contrast with the Church's teaching on sex?

_____

_____

_____

_____

3. Outside of your family, what was your earliest exposure to sex?
   What did the books you read, the music you listened to, and the
   movies you watched teach you about sex in marriage? How does
   this compare and contrast with the Church's teaching on sex?

_____

_____

_____

_____

4. What was the teaching of your religious upbringing about sex in
   marriage? How does this compare and contrast with the Orthodox
   Church's teaching on sex?

_____

_____

_____

_____

5. Read 1 Thessalonians 4:3-7. What limitations does Paul place on
   sexual relations within marriage?

_____

_____

5b. **(For married couples):** Analyze your sexual relations by Saint
   Paul's standards. In what ways do you need to change your
   behavior and/or your thinking?

_____

_____

_____

6. What is your understanding of the Church's teaching on the

following important issues? Be prepared to talk with your priest about these issues.

a. Abortion _____

_____

_____

b. Homosexuality _____

_____

c. Open marriages and/or trial marriages _____

_____

d. Pornography _____

_____

e. Birth control _____

_____

f. Oral copulation _____

_____

g. Appropriate frequency of sexual relations in marriage_____

_____

h. Abstinence in sexual relations _____

_____

i. Masturbation _____

_____

j. Divorce and remarriage _____

_____

7. Do you have any questions about anything relating to marital sexuality which you want to ask your priest? If so, please write them down here and bring them up at your next meeting.

_____

_____

_____

_____

_____

QUESTIONS FOR MARRIED COUPLES ONLY:

1. Chances are your marriage has had its share of disagreement over sexual issues. Think about the root reasons for the conflicts. In what way have these conflicts been fueled by false understandings of sex in marriage? How will adopting a fully Orthodox understanding of sex help you work through them?

_____

_____

_____

_____

2. In many marriages, at least one of the two spouses is disappointed in the sexual aspect of their relationship. There are many different reasons for this, but very often it boils down to differing sexual desires and expectations. It is good to talk about these and discuss them, but even still it is likely that some level of disappointment will remain. Satan will try to exploit this disappointment to make you bitter and resentful or to encourage you to look elsewhere for sexual satisfaction (either to another person or to self-gratification). As Orthodox Christians, it is here that we must embrace the realities of self-denial and self-crucifixion. In Christ's Name we must accept the suffering caused by unfulfilled desire without bitterness, anger, or resentment. If we do, we shall find that the power of Christ's Resurrection can only truly be known in the context of sharing Christ's sufferings. Here the true meaning of the martyr's crowns is revealed to us. We must die to self in our marriages. This may mean that we must die to our sexual desires, cutting off our own will, and submitting ourselves in cheerful

obedience to the will of another. If we do, God promises His peace, His joy, and His victory will be ours.

Think very specifically about this and recommit yourself to your marriage and to walking the way of the cross in your marriage. If you have any questions about this, please jot them down here and talk to your priest about them. He can direct you to spiritual reading which will help to flesh this out. Whatever you do, do not yield to the temptation to satisfy your desires by yourself or with someone else. These roads lead to spiritual ruin!

_____

_____

_____

Notes and comments/ things to discuss:

EPILOGUE

MAKING A PERSONAL STATEMENT OF COMMITMENT

The Orthodox tradition is very insistent upon the importance of people making free decisions. In the marriage ceremony, this is emphasized during the betrothal. Before the actual ceremony begins, the priest questions both the groom and the bride: "Have you with a good, free, and unconstrained will promised to take this woman/man whom you see here to be your wedded wife/husband?" On the negative side, this question is intended to make sure that no one is being forced into a marriage against his or her own will. On the positive side, this question is intended to remind you of your part in establishing the marriage. Marriage is a commitment you make to God, to yourself, and to your spouse. As you reflect on all that you have studied so far in this workbook, read through the following "sample" statement of commitment.

As I marry you, I am making an unchangeable commitment to know and love God and to know and love you. I can learn to love only as I come to know God's love for me. I therefore commit myself to seek Him daily and to allow His love for us to fill me.

I promise never to stop seeking to learn to love you better. I want my love to be patterned after the description found in 1 Corinthians 13. I promise to be patient with your failings, to be kind and persevering, to refrain from jealousy or envy. I promise not to seek to control you, but to allow you the freedom you need to grow and develop into the person God has called you to be. I will endeavor not to be rude or inconsiderate of your needs and desires. I want to be gentle with you and not overpower or domineer over you. Most of all I want you to know of Christ's love for you through me.

I commit myself to seek with God's help to overlook your annoying faults, sins, failings, and inconsistencies, to be glad to forgive you and to remember that I have failed you and irritated you far more often than you have failed or irritated me. I will seek to show you a love that is deeply grieved when you are hurt or troubled and responds to your need with a hand up, not a push down. I promise to restore and uplift rather than demean, despise, expose, or condemn.

By God's grace I resolve to love you with a love that does not demand its own way; a love that is creatively thoughtful and constantly looks for new ways to please and encourage. I promise to put your needs and desires above my own. I will stick by you and protect you regardless of personal cost. I promise to believe the best about you and will seek to put the best interpretations on your deeds and motives.

I enter into this marriage with no preconceived limits to my love or my trust. When others fail or fall away, I will stand by you to the end. I covenant myself to be wholly devoted to you and to pursue an exclusive intimacy with you.

I promise to share with you daily my thoughts, dreams, hopes, joys, successes, troubles, fears, failures—in short, I will keep nothing from you but will open myself fully and unashamedly to your involvement and presence. More than that, I ask you to do the same with me. I am interested in you as a person and in what you think and feel. I want to listen to you, to share with you, and to care about you now and ever and unto ages of ages.

As I enter marriage, I know that I am not capable by myself to fulfill my commitment to you. Therefore I pledge to you and to God to daily pursue my relationship with Him in and through His Holy, Catholic, and Apostolic Church. I, therefore, make all of these commitments with the understanding that I must first of all be committed wholeheartedly to the Father, the Son, and the Holy Spirit; by His grace, that I am, and, by His grace, that I will continue to be. This is my commitment to God and to you.

1. **(For engaged couples:)** Are you willing to make a commitment such as this?

   _____ YES   _____ NO   _____ NOT SURE

   If you have any hesitation at all, please don't pretend it isn't there. Talk about it in the presence of your priest! Now is the time to rethink your decision—not after the ceremony!

2. **(For engaged couples:)** If you answered "YES" to the above question, write out your own commitment statement. (Page 132 is

set aside for this purpose.) When the priest asks you, "Have you . . . promised to take this woman/man . . . to be your wedded wife/husband?" and you say, "I have," what are you promising? Look back over your work in chapters 1 and 2 and write a personal statement to your partner beginning with the words: "As I marry you, I promise . . ." Make your statement personal and specific. You may, of course, use elements from the sample statement, but don't directly copy it. This is your understanding of what marriage is all about. Take the time and spend the energy to develop a statement which you can look back on as your marriage develops.

You will likely fail in living up to all of your promises. And your spouse will undoubtedly fail in living up to all of his/her promises to you. Return to this statement in the years ahead and use it to remind yourselves of your original goals, and to recommit yourselves to your marriage.

3. (**For married couples:**) Now that you have come to the end of this manual, let me strongly suggest that you recommit yourselves to your marriage. Your marriage is of God! God believes in it and so too must you. God has richly given you the grace to experience His love in the context of your marital relationship. You must work with this grace to achieve His design and purpose in your life. To do this requires commitment and perseverance. Put far from you any temptation to bail out or to invest your time and energy in other activities which take you away from your marriage.

Write out your own commitment statement to your spouse. (Page 132 is set aside for this purpose.) Make your statement personal and specific. You may, of course, use elements from the sample statement, but don't directly copy it. This is your understanding of what marriage is all about. If you were married before you joined the Orthodox Church, you may also want to talk to your priest about having your marriage blessed at a special service. Even if you had an Orthodox wedding, do something special to celebrate your marriage and your own commitment to making it work: for now—and for eternity!

My personal commitment statement:

_____

_____

_____

_____

_____

_____

_____

_____

_____

_____

_____

_____

_____

_____

_____

_____

_____

_____

_____

_____

_____

_____

_____

_____

_____

_____

_____

Supplemental Reading Section

HOW TO USE THE SUPPLEMENTAL READING SECTION

With the exception of Supplement A, all of the supplemental readings in this section are drawn from the pages of AGAIN Magazine, a quarterly publication of the Antiochian Orthodox Christian Archdiocese of North America. Conciliar Press has often received requests from priests involved in marital counseling for reprints of these AGAIN articles, and it was in response to these requests that we decided to put these materials together in anthology form.

The following readings are intended to serve as a supplement to the main body of the book. In the case of those who are engaged, they are intended to be used in conjunction with a series of premarital counseling sessions with your priest or other counselor. As you read through the eight main chapters of this book, you will find gray boxes in the margins indicating that supplemental reading on a particular subject is available. While not every chapter has supplemental readings attached to it, most chapters have one or more. Use this supplementary material as a springboard for discussion.

If you find you do not have the time to go through all of the supplemental readings in the time allotted between counseling sessions, ask your priest or counselor which readings would be most applicable to your individual situation. Each of the articles stands alone and has its own discussion questions, so you can come back to them at a later date for continuing "marriage enrichment" sessions with your partner.

GUIDELINES GOVERNING MARRIAGES
IN THE ORTHODOX CHURCH:

CHOOSING A DATE FOR YOUR WEDDING:
The marriage date must be set for those days and seasons approved by the Church for marriage. There are specific times and seasons when marriages cannot be performed:
- during the week before Lent, Great Lent, Holy Week, and Bright Week;
- during the Christmas Fast (from November 15 through Christmas Day), and from Christmas until Theophany (January 6);
- during the Fast of the Theotokos (August 1 through 14);
- during the Fast of the Apostles (second Monday after Pentecost until June 29);
- on the eves of the Lord's Day and of major feasts, and on the days of the great feasts of the Lord;
- the Beheading of John the Baptist (August 28 and 29);
- the Exaltation of the Cross (September 13 and 14);
- all Wednesdays and Fridays unless it is a fast-free period.

A wedding may be celebrated at such times *only* on account of a grave necessity *and* only with special permission of the diocesan bishop.

Also make sure with your priest that there are no other conflicts regarding the day you want to get married (i.e. the church facilities are scheduled for another purpose, the priest is unable to serve on that date, etc.).

DETERMINE IF THERE IS ANY REASON YOU MAY *NOT* BE MARRIED:
There are certain instances in which marriages cannot be performed in the Orthodox Church, due either to closeness of blood relationship or to closeness of spiritual relationship.

Marriages are prohibited between:
- parents with their own children or grandchildren;
- brothers-in-law with sisters-in-law;
- uncles and aunts with nieces and nephews;
- first cousins;
- foster parents with foster children;
- godfather or godmother with godchild;
- godfather with mother of godchild;
- godmother with father of godchild.

Priests must further verify:
- that neither the bride nor bridegroom is already married;
- that if either of the Orthodox parties has been civilly divorced, he/she also has an ecclesiastical ruling recognizing that divorce;

- that if either of the parties is widowed, he or she has a legal death certificate of his or her deceased spouse;
- that both parties have valid baptismal certificates, and are Orthodox Christians in good standing, both sacramentally and in church support [*or* if non-Orthodox, they have been baptized in the name of the Holy Trinity by a recognized Christian communion];
- that this will not be a fourth marriage for either the bride or the groom.

A WORD ABOUT MIXED MARRIAGES:

When either the bride or the groom is not an Orthodox Christian, it is considered a mixed marriage. The Orthodox Church blesses marriages between Orthodox and non-Orthodox Christians only if the non-Orthodox Christian has been baptized in the name of the Holy Trinity, within a recognized Christian communion. In the event the non-Orthodox has not been baptized in the name of the Holy Trinity, the marriage cannot take place in the Orthodox Church. The non-Orthodox person must be willing to be instructed and baptized before the marriage may take place.

An Orthodox wedding must be celebrated by an Orthodox priest, in an Orthodox church, and according to all of the rites and traditions of the Orthodox Church. Non-Orthodox elements may not be added to or incorporated within the Betrothal or Crowning service. Non-Orthodox clergymen may not take part in any of the prayers, readings, or liturgical actions of the Betrothal or Crowning ceremony itself.

If an Orthodox Christian is married outside the Orthodox Church, he excommunicates himself; he is no longer permitted to receive communion, to be a godparent at an Orthodox baptism, or to be a sponsor at an Orthodox wedding.

A non-Orthodox person married to an Orthodox Christian in the Orthodox Church does not automatically become Orthodox as a result of the marriage ceremony. To become Orthodox, the non-Orthodox spouse must still be catechized and chrismated.

LICENSES:

Because of the separation between church and state in America, a civil marriage license is required. The license must be obtained from the city or county clerk's office, in accordance with local laws. No marriage can be performed in the Orthodox Church without the civil license. (Please note: in the Greek Archdiocese, a church license must also be received by petitioning the diocesan bishop through the parish priest.)

SPONSORS, BEST MEN, MAIDS OF HONOR, ETC.:

The sponsor can be either male or female (it is usually the best man), but must be a member of the Orthodox Church in good standing. If married, he or she must have been married in the Orthodox Church. If the sponsor is from another Orthodox parish, a letter must be provided by his or her local parish priest substantiating that he or she is a practicing Orthodox Christian in good standing. The role of the Orthodox sponsor includes being the official witness of the marriage and promising to give the bride and groom moral support throughout their marriage.

In a mixed marriage, if it is the groom who is non-Orthodox, his best man may be non-Orthodox, but in this case the best man is *not* the Orthodox sponsor. For the purposes of the civil license, he can be the second witness to the marriage.

Bridesmaids, groomsmen, ringbearers, and flower girls need not be Orthodox.

SEX

AND THE SPIRIT OF OUR AGE

BY FR. JOHN WELDON HARDENBROOK

S ex: one of the most distorted and grossly misunderstood subjects of the twentieth century. Our society is *obsessed* with sex. You cannot turn on the television, pick up a book or magazine, or go for a drive in your car without being exposed to it.

The results of this obsession are staggering. It has influenced nearly every aspect of our society. Adultery and fornication are rampant. Young people are being marred for life as teenage pregnancies and abortions continue to increase.

Marriages are being destroyed too. There is one divorce for every 1.8 marriages in the United States. Forty percent of children under eighteen have divorced parents. And all too often it is our national preoccupation with and misuse of sex that is at the root of these divorces.

As a priest in the Church and as a father, I am deeply disturbed by this perversion of a God-given gift. It disturbs me because of what it is doing to our world. And it disturbs me because so many Christians are falling prey to it.

As Christians, we should be an example to those around us. Instead, Christians seem to be following the lead of the world. It is time for us to put a stop to that. It is time to put sex back into its proper perspective.

WHEN GOD CREATED SEX . . .

It was the purpose of God to make one man for one woman. A husband and wife were to become one flesh, and their marriage was to last their entire lives. Jesus once said, " 'And the two shall become one flesh'; so then they are no longer two, but one flesh. Therefore what God has joined together, let not man separate" (Mark 10:8, 9).

Thus, the sanctity of marriage is essential to kingdom living. In saying that the two shall become one flesh, Jesus uses words that were used in the Old Testament. The words "one flesh" mean one nature. To be thus joined was not a theoretical union. It was a real union that God ordained. Marriage is, among other things, a physical union.

Sex is vital to the marriage relationship. There are several reasons why this is so. First, sex is necessary for procreation. Second, it provides an intimate form of communication and recreation. Third, and most important for our discussion, sex is one of the instruments that God uses in "making the two one flesh." In other words, sex has the power to help bond people together within a marriage.

Sex was created by God as a good thing. It has a very positive purpose within a marriage. Unfortunately the world has taken this good thing and perverted it.

THE SPIRIT OF THIS AGE

Satan has designed a course for this world called the "spirit of the age." It is not always easy to put your finger on what that spirit is. It is very elusive—

always on the move, always changing. But even with all the changes, a definite progression can be seen. In our generation the progression is becoming more obvious. We can see where at least part of it is leading. It is leading to total rebellion against godly sexual behavior.

This is evidenced by the many forms of pornography that have become readily available and socially acceptable today. Dirty books have put on a new look with glossy four-colored covers, and dirty movies have an "arty" flair.

But perhaps even more insidious are the more subtle ways sex is drummed into our collective consciousness. The advertising industry has splashed sex all over billboards and used it to sell almost everything. The TV and movie industries have made heroes out of sinners. Pop psychology has told us that sex is innocent and natural, and that repressing sexual urges is harmful to our psychological well-being. And the legal system has proclaimed that sex is a "right" among consenting adults.

It is no wonder that what used to be called "living in sin" has become a commonplace, acceptable social option, and that other forms of sexual indulgence are now so prevalent.

THE RESULTS OF THIS OBSESSION ARE STAGGERING.

DON'T BE DECEIVED

I want to give some reasons for not fornicating and not committing adultery. To start with, the Ten Commandments condemn sex outside of marriage. The seventh commandment says, "You shall not commit adultery" (Exodus 20:14). How is that for being clear? That is the Lord speaking. And His law is written on our consciences. People have to fight really hard to harden their hearts to avoid this law.

Secondly, fornicating will send you to hell. It will cost you the Kingdom of God. The Scriptures say, "Do you not know that the unrighteous will not inherit the kingdom of God? Do not be deceived. Neither fornicators . . . nor adulterers . . . will inherit the kingdom of God" (1 Corinthians 6:9, 10). It says "do not be deceived." The world *is* deceived. And someday they're going to come before the throne of God and they're going to say, "But everyone was doing it." So what? Everybody sinned. Everybody was deceived. If you love the Lord, then do not be deceived. It will cost you the Kingdom of God.

Thirdly, fornication and adultery will damage you emotionally and psychologically in this life. Adultery, *adultero* in Latin, means "to give your nature (a foreign nature) to another." This means that when two become one flesh something happens besides just the enjoyment of the moment.

The Bible asks us Christians, "Do you not know that your bodies are members of Christ? Shall I then take the members of Christ and make them members of a harlot? Certainly not! Or do you not know that he who is joined to a harlot is one body with her? For 'the two,' He says, 'shall become one flesh' " (1 Corinthians 6:15, 16). Sex was designed to bring unity within marriage. But outside of marriage, this bonding process becomes a negative thing.

Let's consider a man who has lots of relationships. He has a relationship with girl "A" that is just a one-night stand. Then he has a relationship with girl "B" which lasts a bit longer, say a year. Then he dumps her and has a relationship with girl "C," whom he eventually marries. What is in this man's life? A little bit of "A," a little bit more of "B," and a lot more, hopefully, of "C." Memories, conflicts, and jealousies from each of these relationships will, to some degree, dwell within that one man. He has a little bit of each of them in him. And he left a little bit of himself with each of them too.

We're told by the world that we'll find a fulfilling life through sexual relationships. But the more you practice indiscriminate sex, the more you lose your life.

"BUT WE'LL BE MARRIED SOON ANYWAY"

There are also good reasons to refrain from sex before marriage, even with the one you are sure you are going to marry. Premarital sex builds mistrust. One reason husbands and wives are able to trust each other is because they waited to have sex until they were married. And it was difficult to do. They knew they soon would be married and be living together. They were in love, and they wanted to express that. And it was hard to keep self-disciplined. But people who waited thank God that they did. What was taught during that time of self-discipline and waiting was that if they could wait then, they could also refrain if they were tempted after they got married. Waiting built trust.

The old cliché, "Lust can't wait to get, but love can wait to give," isn't a bad one after all. Engaging in sex might seem a good way of expressing "love," but waiting is a more loving thing to do. Once you've had a premarital sexual relationship, you can never be sure that you can fully trust your partner or yourself again. I've seen this issue come up in marriages even years after couples exchanged wedding vows.

Premarital sex also leaves you open to rejection. Sex is one of the most vulnerable things you can do in your life. You are made to be vulnerable and ten-

der in that moment, not hard-hearted. If that girl or guy leaves you after having sex with you, it does something. You feel rejected. Walls start coming up. And pretty soon you're saying, "I'm not going to get hurt again." And then, years later when you are married, you have a hard time letting go. What is wrong? Subconsciously, you are still thinking, "I may get hurt. I need to protect myself." These premarital relationships cost you. They stay with you.

FLEE IMMORALITY

You've been told sins are no different. One is the same as another. Don't kid yourself. They are different in their effect on you. How can I prove this? "He who is joined to the Lord is one spirit with Him. [But] flee sexual immorality. Every sin that a man does is outside the body, but he who commits sexual immorality sins against his own body" (1 Corinthians 6:17, 18).

What is Paul saying here? If you rob a bank, you can give the money back. But not so with immorality. It goes right into your soul and you can't take it back.

It is common today that people getting married have had sex before marriage. If you are a Christian, and that happened to you, I don't want you to get under a pile of guilt. I'll explain later how healing and forgiveness from the Lord can work in your life.

But do you see what we are after? We want single people to enter into marriage in purity, without carrying in a lot of problems from their past. We want that for our daughters. We want to see them, virginal, in white dresses at their weddings. And we want purity for our sons and for all the young people in our churches.

This will not be easy in our culture because there is so much encouragement to follow the world's attitudes toward sex. There will need to be positive role models in our churches for the young men and women to follow. We need couples who can stand on their wedding day and unashamedly say, "We are virgins," even if it is not the "cool" thing to say.

PRIMING THE PUMP

American culture caters to sinful passions by making necking and petting acceptable behavior. Even in circles where premarital sex is still taboo, there is the attitude that it is O.K. to do everything leading up to intercourse as long as you stop short of that act. What is wrong with necking and petting among single people in dating situations? Let me ask this: what are necking and petting for?

If you were raised in the country or have grandparents that were, you probably know something about "priming the pump." In order to get water from a pump, you have to put a little bit of water in it, and crank away. It takes awhile to get the thing going. You prime the pump to get the water.

What do necking and petting accomplish? They prime the pump. They exist to get things going sexually. And it is a great thing, *in marriage,* to get things going. But such pump-priming has no place whatsoever outside of a sanctified marriage.

How many adults, both single and married, have gotten themselves into trouble right at this point? What starts out as an "innocent" touch leads to not-so-innocent passion, and soon turns into uncontrollable lust. The end result is always the same—broken lives, broken marriages, and estrangement from God.

For young people it is equally tragic, even if necking and petting do not end in fornication. Why? Because it destroys the proper functions of sex that God intended.

Necking and petting were meant to stir things up in an exciting way! Goosebumps and all these sorts of things happen. And it is fun and wonderful. But it was made so that you could finish the course! I'm not talking about little pats and a peck on the cheek. I'm talking about necking and petting. Their purpose is to arouse.

Some people I have counseled have experienced problems from this starting and stopping of the passions. After marriage, they wonder why they can't follow through sexually. When I ask them about their dating patterns, they'll say, "We would be hot and heavy until the last minute. Then we'd stop and try to wind back down." If you keep doing that, it will foul you up when you get married. Your body was not meant to shut down at that point. You're left frustrated.

Many young people today live with constant sexual frustration. This is especially true for dating couples who are necking and petting, who continue to stir up their passions. Now, a certain amount of sexual tension can perhaps be expected by singles. But necking and petting are exceptionally frustrating, and make things more difficult. It is frustrating when you can't finish what you start.

If you don't want to finish I would ask, "Why get started at all?" Don't even start priming the pump. Don't tempt yourself by getting your passions aroused. Why bring on frustration needlessly?

> **WHAT STARTS AS AN "INNOCENT" TOUCH LEADS TO NOT-SO-INNOCENT PASSION.**

I'll tell you who really has fun on the marriage night. The one who fasted. Fasting always make the feast so enjoyable. And singleness is a time for fasting. What excitement is there in the wedding night if the couple says, "Well, this will be just like last night and a lot of other nights we've had"?

The wedding night of two virgins is a wonderful thing. They don't need counselors. They don't suffer from the lack of experience sexually. Why? Because they can't make a mistake. I mean, they have fifty years to figure it out. And it is fun figuring it out. It really is. And over the years their sex life will get better and better.

BUT I'VE ALREADY MADE MISTAKES . . .

So what happens if you've been one of those who have had a lot of bad relationships, or have had sex before marriage? Well, the Lord is our Savior. And He is a healer. This redemption He brings to us can bring great healing to our damaged lives.

I want to be very honest, though. If you cut off your thumb, and you come into the Kingdom of God, most likely you won't get another thumb put on. Now, the Lord *can* do that. But in all likelihood, it won't happen. Yet you can do really well. You may not have a thumb, but you can do a lot. This is sort of what happens with our emotions.

Sometimes with pre- and extra-marital sex experiences in our past, we come into the Kingdom finding that we have a few little pieces missing. That is all right. But it is not as good as it would have been had we not had those relationships.

The difference is that it is a little harder for one who has had such experiences to live the Christian life. We tend to have to fight and struggle against repeating past sins. The temptation is greater. Satan knows it, and he knocks on that same door. It is a little harder, but you can make it.

Life is harder, but the Lord is gracious. He talks to the Corinthians and says, "Neither fornicators . . . nor adulterers . . . will inherit the kingdom of God. . . . And such were some of you." Theirs was a wild church, you know. In the very center of that town was a huge shrine for pagan worship which had several hundred prostitutes as part of the worship. "Such were some of you. But you were washed, but you were sanctified, but you were justified in the name of the Lord Jesus and the Spirit of our God" (1 Corinthians 6:9-11).

That is good news! As you partake of the Lord's Body and Blood weekly, as you progress in your Christian life, and as you become more and more conformed to the image of Christ, healing will take place in your very soul. You can be washed whiter than snow and, as it were, stand before the Lord as a virgin again. The Lord is gracious in these things, and over a period of time will heal you. However, let's be fair to our children and confess that the Christian life is made harder to live because we do reap what we sow.

THE WAR OF TWO KINGDOMS

We are fighting a war. If you think that life is anything other than a war, or that Christians are somehow supposed to have an easy time of things, you'd better reread 1 Peter 5:8. Satan is a roaring lion. He is vicious and without mercy. He has been warring against God since the Fall, and will use anything within his grasp to destroy God's people and His Kingdom.

It is time for Christians to reexamine their attitudes towards sexuality, and to stop being influenced by the unhealthy spirit of this age. That spirit comes directly from Satan, and leads to destruction. Be on guard against it! Do not be taken in by it! Ungodly sexual behavior is a tool of the enemy, and it has been used countless times by him. Let us all pay heed to the warning given to the young man of Proverbs chapter 7, for this wicked twentieth century is calling to us with that same adulteress' call.

> "Come, let us take our fill of
>   love until morning;
> Let us delight ourselves with love.
> For my husband is not at home;
> He has gone on a long journey;
> He has taken a bag of money
>   with him,
> And will come home on the
>   appointed day."
> With her enticing speech she
>   caused him to yield,
> With her flattering lips she
>   seduced him.
> Immediately he went after her,
>   as an ox goes to the slaughter,
> Or as a fool to the correction of
>   the stocks,
> Till an arrow struck his liver.
> As a bird hastens to the snare,
> He did not know it would cost
>   his life.
> Now therefore, listen to me, my
>   children;
> Pay attention to the words of
>   my mouth:
> Do not let your heart turn aside
>   to her ways,
> Do not stray into her paths;
> For she has cast down many
>   wounded,
> And all who were slain by her
>   were strong men.
> Her house is the way to hell,
> Descending to the chambers of
>   death.
>   (Proverbs 7:18-27)

Fr. John W. Hardenbrook
Editor, AGAIN Magazine

From AGAIN Vol. 7, No. 2.
Original publication date: June, 1984

Questions for thought and discussion (for engaged couples):

1)   Outline in your own words the three reasons given for not fornicating or committing adultery, especially explaining how fornication will damage a person emotionally and psychologically.

2)   Using the analogy of "priming the pump," discuss how necking and petting stir up passions and lead to sexual frustration when not allowed to reach their natural conclusion. Decide now how you plan to deal with this in your premarital relationship.

3)   If you are *not* both entering into your marriage as virgins, discuss the extra problems you may have to face, and how to find spiritual healing.

Questions for thought and discussion (for married couples):

1) Think back to your own sexual activity before marriage. Did your courtship meet God's design as outlined in this article? If not, how do you think that "brokenness" has entered your marriage? How has it created problems for you and your spouse? If there was sexual sin in your courtship, it is vitally important for you and your marriage that you confess this as sin and repent of it. Call your priest immediately, and schedule a time for confession.

INTERVIEW

FR. JOHN MEYENDORFF

Marriage

as Sacrament

AGAIN: Marriage is and has been a universal practice for almost every civilized culture throughout history. Why is it then considered to be a sacrament in the Orthodox Church?

FR. JOHN MEYENDORFF: The first question we must address is, what is a sacrament? The word *sacrament* means literally *mystery*. A sacrament is an open door through which mankind passes from the realm of the physical, into the reality of the Spirit—the realm of communion with God. A sacrament is always seen through the context of created reality (for example, red wine in the Eucharist, or water in baptism). This created reality is then projected into the Kingdom of God and transformed into a higher reality which belongs to the eternal realm.

Now, let's apply that definition to marriage. Marriage is, on one level, a created reality which, as you have said, is indeed a universal practice. Men and women are attracted to each other, fall in love, and marry—this is a well-known phenomenon and a reality of the world

as God has created it. But on the other hand, the Church also considers marriage to be a sacrament, a mystery of Christ and the Church, as Ephesians chapter 5 says.

In other words, the created reality of marriage can be assumed into the Kingdom of God and sanctified and continued there. It is not something profane or only secular. When a man and woman come to the Church to be married, they are expressing their desire to transfigure their marriage on earth into the reality of the Kingdom. The transfiguration which takes place is indeed a very profound one. When the Son of God took on human flesh, He ceased to be only Himself, but became also man so that mankind could be joined to His Body. Similarly, a man and a woman cease being two people upon marriage, but in a very real way, become one single flesh. In this act they enter into the mystery of God's salvation of the human race and participate in His redemptive plan.

AGAIN: So a wedding isn't just a private or family affair which only

When a man and woman come to the Church to be married,
they are expressing their desire to
transfigure their marriage on earth into the reality of the Kingdom.
The transfiguration which takes place
is indeed a very profound one.

---

parenthetically takes place in the context of a church. Something extraordinary occurs in the wedding liturgy which would not take place apart from it?

FR. JOHN: Yes, I believe so. Of course a sacrament is not magic. It is a gift of the Holy Spirit, which always must be followed by human cooperation—by men and women living up to the gift of the Holy Spirit which has been bestowed upon them. Even when performed in the context of a Church service, the sacrament of marriage is a gift which requires cooperation.

The reasons for marriage outside the context of the Christian Church are of course based upon other considerations. In the Old Testament, for instance, the predominant view was that one survives through begetting children and that one's life continues in the children. Marriage from that standpoint was seen as a vehicle for the continuation of the race. By this act the promise to Abraham and many others was fulfilled in the coming of Christ as a descendant of Abraham. But in the New Testament, as Ephesians 5 tells us, a radically different aspect of marriage appears. Marriage is not just seen as a tool to get children, but also as something which is shared by a man and a woman who are able to find together the mystery of the Kingdom of God.

This relationship is expressed beautifully in the Scriptures. In the New Testament, the Lord Jesus Himself speaks often of the Kingdom of God as being a wedding feast. And even in the Old Testament, marriage is used to depict God's unique covenantal relationship with His people. The book known as the Song of Songs is actually a love song, but it is a part of the canon because it reveals that in the mutual love of a man and a woman the mystery of the Kingdom of God can be seen.

AGAIN: You have said that Christian marriage is essentially "... a meeting of two beings in love, a human love which can be transformed, by the sacramental grace of the Holy Spirit, into an eternal bond, indissoluble even by death." Could you explain this?

FR. JOHN: As a sacrament, marriage is more than a legal contract and a pledge of a mutual faithfulness and support between two people while they are on earth. A legal contract is interrupted by death. But because a Christian marriage belongs to the Kingdom of God, it is implicitly an eternal bond which will continue on into eternity. In the sacrament of marriage, the boundaries between heaven and earth are broken. Human decision and action acquire an eternal dimension.

Of course at this point the question always comes up concerning Jesus' conversation with the Sadducees in Mark chapter 12. Why does He tell them that in the resurrection men neither marry nor are given in marriage but are as the angels in heaven?

Let's remember the context of this

Divorce is something which is
utterly discouraged in the Orthodox Church.
At best it is considered as an abnormality.

passage. Christ is dialoguing with the Sadducees concerning the resurrection of the dead. The Sadducees, of course, denied the resurrection. To prove their point, they had raised a hypothetical question to Jesus. What about a woman who was married seven times on earth, to seven brothers? Whose wife would she be in heaven?

The Sadducees were actually making two mistakes. First, and most obviously, they were grossly mistaken in denying the resurrection. But secondly, they were also mistaken in their view of marriage. According to their understanding, marriage was nothing more than an instrument of procreation. Certainly, they thought, no one could believe that such an earthly institution would be worthy of God's eternal Kingdom.

With this in mind, we see that our Lord was actually refuting both heresies in His statement to the Sadducees. Yes, there will indeed be a resurrection, but no, marriage as the Sadducees understood it—a mere tool for bodily contact which results in child-bearing—will not exist. We must not take His statement farther than it was intended to go. The New Testament clearly teaches that marriage is more than procreative in design. Marriage is the mystical union of two beings created in God's image, and is an icon of the relationship between Christ and His Church (Ephesians 5). As such, it can and does assume an eternal dimension. Christ's words to the Sadducees do not in any way contradict what the Scriptures consistently teach about the sacramentality of marriage.

Clearly the early Church understood marriage in this eternal sense. This can be seen from the decisive way in which the canons of the Church depart from an Old Testament understanding of death and remarriage. In the Old Testament you find the so-called law of the Levirate, in which the brother of a man who died was supposed to take his wife and restore the seed of his brother. In the passage cited above, the Jews carry this out to an extreme: What if, because of this law of the Levirate, a woman is married seven times? Whose wife will she be in the resurrection?

Quite to the contrary, the canon law of the Church is directed at discouraging remarriages. The thought of marrying seven times is something which is absolutely unthinkable in the Christian Church according to the canon law and also according to the Tradition. The point of the resurrection, as Jesus explained to the Jews, is not whether we will go on begetting children in heaven. Rather it is about the unity of the two beings— that is the primary, the first priority, precisely because it is eternal, and therefore is not even interrupted by death. So it is very clear that it is a kind of Old Testament versus New Testament emphasis which is at stake.

AGAIN: Can you amplify a bit on the Orthodox position concerning divorce and remarriage?

FR. JOHN: Divorce is something which is utterly discouraged in the Orthodox Church. At best it is considered as an abnormality. But as with many of the deficiencies of our Christian life, divorce is treated within the penitential structure of the Church. It is handled with understanding (more understanding in some cases than in others), with love, and with concern. Although we look upon marriage as indissoluble, there are cases where it is dissolved—cases where one of the partners disappears without a trace, cases of insanity. The reasons why marriage simply does not exist are numerous.

This is why, for lay people, remarriage is permitted and understood as a second chance, or even a third chance in some cases. Second and third marriages are not permitted for the clergy, however. Somebody who is married twice, or even who is married to somebody who has been married before, canonically ceases to be a candidate for ordination. This is so not because it is a danger for his salvation, but because if he is in the ministry he should act as an example and follow the norm.

A person doesn't need to be a bishop or a priest or a deacon to be saved. One needs to be a Christian to be saved, and the Church is concerned about securing people's salvation. If in certain cases someone is not eligible to be a minister or a priest, then so be it. There are many other avenues of service available to him.

AGAIN: Roman Catholic tradition differs from Orthodox tradition at this point. Catholic priests are not allowed to marry at all while Orthodox priests can be married, but only one time. Why does this discrepancy exist?

FR. JOHN: In my recent book on Church history, I have a whole chapter on the origins of the celibate priesthood within the West. This teaching began to appear very early, starting in the fourth century. And the basis of it seems to have been double. On the one hand, there is the Augustinian idea that sex, and sexual relations as such, belong to the fallen world and are sinful. The thought here is that consecrated beings should not engage in worldly behavior.

The other half of the teaching is based on the levitical regulations found in the Old Testament. According to these regulations, before offering sacrifices in the temple in Jerusalem, priests were to be continent. Because in the West Mass was often celebrated daily, this idea of ritual purity meant that a priest must be celibate.

Now in the East, you do not have that emphasis. There was always the teaching that on the eve of participating in the Eucharist one should observe continence. That idea exists in the East. But the reasons for it have nothing to do with ritual impurity or anything of that sort. Rather, they are based on the same regulations as those of fasting from food before taking the Eucharist. In both cases what is involved is a preparation for the coming of Christ—a kind of eschatological expectation which is better preserved by an attitude of sobriety and prayer.

So finally, the Orthodox Church considers that a man who is married and has a normal family life is perfectly eligible for the priesthood. I believe that this is normal and goes back to the early Church.

AGAIN: And whether clergy or lay person, the ideal would be for a man and woman to remain married

The Church is very explicit in saying that children are a normal and God-established consequence of marriage. However . . . the Orthodox Church has never stood against a rational, responsible attitude towards birth control in its acceptable forms.

throughout their lifetime and, after death separates them, for the surviving spouse to wait in chastity to be reunited with the other spouse?

FR. JOHN: That is correct. Everything else is a condescension to particular situations. Saint Paul allows, and even encourages, the remarriage of widowers. Allowances must also be permitted because there are marriages which are a mistake. We have teenage marriages, we have forced marriages, we have cases where the marriage was clearly a mistake. In some cases marriage, being a gift of God, was not truly received. And so a second chance is offered. And I believe that this is the way the Church approaches the idea of multiple marriages.

In the West, in the Roman Catholic Church particularly, the whole emphasis is placed upon the legal nature of marriage as a contract between two freely choosing parties. The world around considers this contract on a temporal level. It's based on the mutual consent of the two parties. When this consent does not exist, the contract is broken. In the Roman Catholic tradition this contract is seen to be indissoluble, thus making divorce impossible apart from annulment. So the emphasis of the Roman Catholic tradition is on the juridical nature of the contract, whereas in the Orthodox tradition, the emphasis is on the eschatological, eternal character of marriage as an ideal, and a recognition that the ideal is not always realized.

AGAIN: Let's talk for a moment about the ramifications of the Orthodox view of marriage in the practical area of family planning.

FR. JOHN: As I said earlier, the meaning of marriage is to be found in the union of the two persons according to the image of the union of God and Israel, Christ and the Church, and so on. That is central. Now on the other hand, having children is a great thing, is a blessing, and the Church is very explicit in saying that children are a normal and God-established consequence of marriage.

However, at no time did the Church condone, as the Jews would have before Christ, divorce in cases of infertility. A childless couple is no *less* obligated to mutual faithfulness than a couple with children. This points to the fact that their union is first priority, of which childbirth is a blessed, but not necessary, consequence.

There is a specific text in the writings of Saint John Chrysostom which contrasts the two visions of marriage in the Old and the New Testament. He says that according to the Old Testament, a woman who is sterile can be abandoned. Whereas in the New Testament, Saint Chrysostom says specifically that we are primarily concerned about the new birth, the birth from the font of baptism; that is the true birth, and therefore the birth of many children is not an end in itself anymore.

So in view of it all I think that the Orthodox Church has never stood against a rational, responsible attitude towards birth control in its acceptable forms. The Church doesn't try to make any false

When the pro-abortion movement
attempts to justify itself by claiming that abortion
is a human right or a woman's right,
it ignores human responsibility and becomes quite inhumane.

distinctions between what is "natural" and what is "unnatural" in terms of birth control. A so-called "natural" method of birth control by abstention from sexual intercourse is still a form of birth control, whether we want to call it that or not. And it's not any more "natural" than other methods, since there is nothing "natural" about a husband and wife staying apart from each other.

In the area of family planning, then, I think that Orthodoxy offers both a degree of freedom and responsibility. These follow from the overall understanding of marriage in the Orthodox Church.

AGAIN: What about abortion?

FR. JOHN: Here, of course, it's very clear. The Orthodox Church believes that human life begins at conception. Otherwise why would we celebrate the Feast of the Annunciation, the feast which marks the conception of Christ in the womb of the Virgin Mary? When Joseph looked at Mary with a secular eye, and thought that this was a girl in trouble, he wanted to "put her away privately," as we hear in the Gospel. He didn't turn to abortion.

So it's clear, therefore, that the Church and Scripture consider that the life has begun. Therefore, interrupting pregnancy is killing—there is no way we can escape from it. Now the Church has never been systematically and universally pacifist. It has never been universally against capital punishment. It has allowed killing in certain cases—self-defense, as at war, and there are military saints.

But the Church has never said that killing was good. Killing was always killing. So the important thing about abortion is that it is not a question of a woman's free choice. It is a question of killing. Once she recognizes that this is a killing then let her choose. But she must realize that what she chooses is a great evil. If the abortion is clearly to save the life of the mother, a decision must be made in favor of the lesser evil. Even in such cases it is never a question of human rights. No human being has the right to kill.

What deeply bothers me about the current debate over the issue of abortion is that the argument is based solely around the issue of rights. While Orthodoxy recognizes the importance of human freedom, it also recognizes the responsibility that goes along with that freedom. When the pro-abortion movement attempts to justify itself by claiming that abortion is a human right or a woman's right, it ignores human responsibility and becomes quite inhumane.

AGAIN: What does Christ's attendance at the wedding at Cana (John chapter 2) teach us concerning the sanctity and value of marriage—especially in light of the high view of monasticism and celibacy which is so apparent in the teaching of the Church?

FR. JOHN: There is something about early Christianity which tends, even in the New Testament with Saint Paul, to exalt celibacy and continence even at the expense of marriage. The early Church, even before Constantine, is dominated by this exaltation of celibacy, and then afterwards comes monasticism. If you take the patristic literature as a whole, you'll have an immense volume of writing justifying celibacy and a relatively small volume of texts about marriage.

While not in any way denying the validity of this New Testament and patristic emphasis on celibacy as a calling for some, we must never ignore the counterbalance which is also present in the Church's Tradition. For example, you have many Fathers of the Church, particularly the great Saint John Chrysostom, who are so explicit about the value of marriage and the family. And then also in the fourth century the Council of Gangra flatly condemns those who are against marriage.

Last but not least, you have the Scripture where Jesus went to a wedding; and as our liturgy of the wedding service says, He sanctified marriage simply by being there. This passage of Scripture highly exalts the sanctity of marriage. It is a clear endorsement of marriage and is a strong text to explain why marriage is understood to be a sacrament by the catholic and universal teaching of the Church. I believe the John chapter 2 passage, the first of the signs performed by Jesus according to the Gospel of John, is also symbolic. The transformation of water into wine is symbolic of the sacramental transformation of earthly reality into something eternal.

In addition to having been the Dean of Saint Vladimir's Orthodox Seminary and professor of Patristics and Church History, Father Meyendorff was also the author of many books, including Marriage: An Orthodox Perspective *(St. Vladimir's Seminary Press, 1984).*

Fr. Meyendorff died in 1992. May his memory be eternal!

From AGAIN Vol. 13, No. 2.
Original publication date: June, 1990

Questions for thought and discussion:

1) Father Meyendorff states that the Orthodox wedding ceremony is more than the execution of a legal contract, and that marriage is more than a vehicle for the continuation of the human race. Discuss together the implications of the sacramental view of marriage. What does it mean to you:

  a) that by your marriage you become one flesh;
  b) that your marriage is an icon of the relationship between Christ and the Church;
  c) that in your marriage you enter into the mystery of God's salvation of the human race; and
  d) that your marriage is eternal?

2) Discuss together your understanding of the Orthodox viewpoint on divorce. How do you reconcile the fact that the Orthodox Church utterly discourages divorce, and yet permits second and third marriages? When may marriages be dissolved? What are the implications of the statement that "divorce is treated within the penitential structure of the Church"?

Marriage & Family as Sacrament

BY FR. GREGORY C. WINGENBACH

The Age of Aquarius is gone for good. Long live the Age of the Family!

For Western society in general, and America in particular, the tide of rugged individualism and selfish independence has finally begun to recede. No longer does society judge the benefits of a social institution solely by the criterion, "What's in it for me?" No longer do the "me-first" values of the tumultuous sixties and yuppie-oriented seventies hold center stage.

Today, even the United Nations is planning an "International Year of Family and Families." Sociological studies emphasize the critical necessity of wholesome family life. And national and local election campaigns have placed the family and traditional values as the "make or break" issue for politicians.

For Christians, the vital importance of the family can never be overemphasized, as long as it does not overshadow the role of God in our lives. We might welcome this new opportunity to deepen our understanding about family life and its centrality to our society, but the importance of the family cannot—or at least should not—come as a surprise. After all, it is God Himself who established marriage as the very basis of human society.

In Genesis 2:18, we find the words: "And the LORD God said, 'It is not good that man should be alone; I will make him a helper comparable to him' " Here is a three-way covenant—of God, man, and woman. Through this covenant, which mirrors the unity of the Divine Trinity, man and woman are no longer separate individuals, nor are they alone.

In fidelity to that divine covenant which the Creator made with man, woman, and their progeny, the very Son of God became the Messiah in this world. The Son of God was born humbly of a woman who was and remains the epitome of her sex, "the crowning glory of womanhood," as one of the more poetic Church Fathers was to call the Theotokos, Blessed Virgin Mary.

In the course of His earthly ministry, the Son of Man forever righted the relationship of man and woman. In sharp contrast to all the ancient prejudices, He proceeded to consecrate the human act of male/female union. As a hallowed act of the Body of Christ, instead of being merely a civil contract or temporal arrangement for the sake of the state and secular order, marriage consecrates the

Marriage and family are
the school for life,
the micro-cosmos that contains within itself
"the mustard seed of the Kingdom."

man and the woman together to God and unto one another. They are strengthened for constant celebration.

THE HOME:
A SCHOOL FOR LIFE

Throughout the course of human history, God has always gone directly to the roots and heart of the human condition—acting together with, in the midst of, and using the very elements of humankind, nature, and history. God's acts are incarnational and relevant to us. He most often works through the ordinary and the material, rather than grandiose schemes or incredible feats of magic, to effect change and give meaning to life. The supreme example of this principle of divine action is the Son of Man's own life, death, and ministry in this world.

Marriage and family are the most commonplace of human situations, the first and most basic community of all. Marriage and family are the place where all of humankind's—man's and woman's, children's and adolescents'—proclivities, strengths and weaknesses, hopes and fears, sinning against one another, learning to love and care for "the other," failing and succeeding, and just being human have the chance to take place. By contrast, the world "outside" is more quick to pounce, to rule, to judge and quantify, and doesn't easily allow such an openness and gradual coming into being.

Marriage and family are sacred because the drama and events of life take place and unfold there. Not so the world, where social priorities and temporary trends take precedence over the struggling individual. Marriage and family are where—more than anywhere else—the free-acting grace of God and faith, hope, and love must be. The example of the servant-Christ is the model here—or else there is no marriage, no family, no household, no "brethren dwelling together in unity" (Psalm 133:1), and no future.

It is here that we as human beings can "let down our hair" and take off the masks that otherwise keep us from intimacy. Here we can see our most primal emotions mirrored in another's equally vulnerable eyes, as well as voice apparently absurd kinds of dreams and hopes, trustingly, without fear of ridicule, put-down, or betrayal. Needless to say, these benefits are ours if the family relationship is itself trustworthy and healthy.

Marriage and family are, then, the school for life, the micro-cosmos that contains within itself "the mustard seed of the Kingdom" (Mark 4:26-32). Marriage and family hold up before a too often insensitive society the ideal by which men, women, and children can truly live, not just exist. Perhaps this is why the Apostle Paul speaks of marriage and family, consecrated in God, as a "great mystery" (Ephesians 5:32, 33). He goes even further to say that marriage touches on—contains within itself—the very nature of the relationship between Christ and His Church.

RECLAIMING SEXUALITY

No doubt that is why the blessed Church Father John Chrysostom reacted so indignantly when both contemporary libertines and some of those teaching within the Church tended to reduce marriage to the animal level, when they characterized the very human sexual and spiritual relationships between a man and a woman as something to be regarded as "a necessary evil . . . something tainted . . . allowable for the sole sake of procreating offspring." In righteous anger, he said, "I am disgusted; for the very gift of God, the root of our generation, has been insulted. Let us cleanse our discourse on this subject and see marriage pure and noble, as God created it, for only in that way can we stop the mouths of heretics. . ." (Homily 12 on Colossians).

Yet that very attitude which Chrysostom condemned is a theme present within certain elements of both Eastern and Western Christian tradition, persisting to this very day, and it has frequently hedged, circumscribed, and unnaturally demeaned the marriage relationship and human sexuality by rules and notions artificially constructed and ungraciously arrived at.

Such attitudes are extremely harmful, for they betray our fundamental feelings. They teach and prophesy—rightly or wrongly as the case may be—the world that is to be. Do husband and wife treat their relationship wearily as a "duty"? Do they treat their love-making and human sexuality as unmentionable facts of life "decent folks" just don't talk about, thus giving a negative witness to their children and each other?

Such attitudes also betray that we are, nevertheless, titillated by the world's distorted and often sordid portrayal of sex—instead of appreciating it as something which God Himself designed to be the most beautiful expression of human intimacy, something that is indeed wonderful and sacred. Such will also be the attitudes of our children, who may very well feel they have to seek artificial intimacy and excitement outside of marriage and family, just as the Victorian generations did.

Do husband and wife strike out at each other's vulnerability, even in slighting little ways which show a lack of respect for "the other"? So will our children! Do husband and wife put social, career, and recreational interests and ambitions ahead of marriage, family, and human needs? So will our children!

In all of this, the net effect will be that marriage and family will drop more than just a notch in our children's estimation and planning for the future. *Kat' oikon ekklesia* ("the Church in/of the Home"), as Saint Paul liked to characterize it (see Romans 16:5, 1 Corinthians 16:19, Colossians 4:15), will come to be perceived as just another convenient societal living arrangement, another fact of life to be endured rather than rejoiced over and lived.

What it often adds up to is the modern phenomena of child runaways, breakdown of parent/teen communication and mutual respect, youthful despair and alienation, and aberrant misbehavior. Ultimately, the children of such marriages are "grown up" only in physique, becoming self-centered adults—children who act out rather than actually live marriage and family. Thus they become part of the tragic human statistics of abuse, divorce, and broken homes. History is repeated, not improved, in this tragic cycle.

Marriage and family are a sacrament of life, because they are where the "unseen warfare of the soul" (*cf.* Ephesians 6:12-17, 1 Timothy 1:18, 19) is fought. Above all, they are where the "holy things" that matter in life can and ought to be present. The very word and notion

> *"Let us cleanse our discourse on this subject*
> *and see marriage pure and noble,*
> *as God created it,*
> *for only in that way can we stop the mouths of heretics. . ."*
> —*St. John Chrysostom*

of "sacrament" derives from the most basic elements of life: the Latin *sacra,* "holy things," and the Greek *menoun,* "live/abide/persist." Thus "sacrament" is the place, the state of being, where the "holy things" that matter in life can and ought to be present. Here is where above all the holy ones, by the grace of God, dwell and have their being in His covenant. Now we see more clearly why the Apostle liked calling marriage and family life *kat' oikon ekklesia*—the Church in/of the Home. For this, so far as he was concerned, is where the very Liturgy of Life begins and continues, day by day and in every land.

GARDEN OF THE SOUL

In basic human terms, what can all this possibly mean? First of all, we frequently use the Greek/Latin words "family" and "sacrament" to describe the married state. Obviously, family denotes and involves the "familiar," the most ordinary of relationships common to life. In demotic Greek, it becomes *oikogeneia*—that is, the things that are of the most basic origin, those which get to our very roots and generate life, flesh, and blood anew out of what came before, within the context of a common household. Likewise, derivatively and theologically, "sacrament" involves those basic elements and doings of human life which, in God, are somehow transfigured with new purpose and being, in order that Christ can "take flesh and dwell among us."

Marriage, the male/female relationship, the household are that elementary stuff upon which the very fabric of both the human community and the Kingdom depend. This includes:

Persons—expressing the diversity of gifts in personhood.

Faithfulness—keeping promises, showing trust.

Truthfulness—maintaining an attitude of openness and honesty.

Community—living, giving, and sharing together.

Communication—talking, listening, and hearing.

Cooperation—the two-way street of working life out together.

Accepting responsibility—putting aside the easy solution, avoiding temptation no matter how attractive or personally advantageous.

Healing—reaching out to the other when he or she falls or is hurt.

Humility—acting so that another may not feel or be humiliated.

Love—But, most of all, to quote the Apostle, **"the greatest of these is love"** (see 1 Corinthians 12:31—13:13) and the making and sustaining thereof by the partners, helpmates in marriage.

Obviously, these are all very homey, ordinary virtues and ways of behaving. But, without them, the human relationship and social contract itself crumble, for these very ordinary virtues are also the attributes of the Divine, necessary to the very sustaining of life. That is precisely why marriage and family are sacred. They are "Thy Gifts of Thine Own," the things of life that we offer in the Holy of Holies, out of what God has given to us in this world.

It is appropriate, then, to conclude with a quote from Saint Gregory Nazianzus—a priest and bishop who came from a clerical family which was not without its own share of life's problems: "So you fear to marry, surmising that you will somehow be corrupted by the flesh? Fear not this consecration of flesh unto flesh: know, rather, that by this act of marriage you will be pure" (Oration 40:18 on Holy Baptism).

Of such is the Kingdom of heaven!

After a sixteen-year secular career in journalism, government, and education, Father Wingenbach was ordained to the priestly ministry of the Greek Orthodox Church in 1971. He has pastored communities in America and Greece, as well as serving the Church in ecumenical assignments. He holds a secular and a theological bachelor's degree, a master of divinity, and a doctorate in pastoral and ecumenical theology. Presently the Greek Orthodox Archdiocese's National Director of Family Life Ministries, he is married, with four children.

From AGAIN Vol. 12, No. 1.
Original publication date: March, 1989

Questions for thought and discussion:

1) Discuss how marriage and family can serve as a "school for life." How will you consciously create an atmosphere in your new home that will allow you to be vulnerable and to "let down your hair"? How will you create an atmosphere in your new home that will encourage the growth of grace, faith, hope, and love in each other's life, and where the example of the servant-Christ is the model?

2) Discuss the attitudes and feelings you have towards married sexuality. Do you see sexuality as "a necessary evil . . . allowable for the sole sake of procreating offspring," or as an "unmentionable fact of life" decent folks don't talk about? Do you see married sexuality as something "pure and noble" which "God Himself designed to be the most beautiful expression of human intimacy, something that is indeed wonderful and sacred"? Or do you have mixed and competing feelings? To what degree did your parents' view of sexuality shape your own attitudes; to what degree did American society and the media shape your attitudes?

3) Think of specific examples of how marriage and family can help you practice each of the following virtues: faithfulness, truthfulness, community, communication, cooperation, accepting responsibility, healing, humility, and love.

The Arena of ☩ Marriage

By Fr. Marc Dunaway

For the vast majority of Christians marriage and family life are the arena where God will chisel away the rough edges of their fallen nature and make them ready for reshaping in His own image and likeness.

From the window of the church office a single light spills into a quiet night. But inside the room a battle rages. The wife explodes, "He doesn't love me. He treats me like one of his customers. All he cares about is his work!" She sobs into a tissue. The husband retorts, "She won't get her hooks out of me! Nothing makes her happy. Maybe I should just move out." The priest, tense, but accustomed to such conflict, waiting to speak, inwardly prays that he can help them.

Is this the bitter end of a Christian marriage already ten years old? Or is it the critical beginning for a new stage not only of marital, but of personal spiritual growth as well? By the grace of God and with the commitment and effort of both husband and wife, it will be the latter.

Such a volatile scene is not uncommon. Most marriages will have their share of explosive battles along with a good portion of routine conflicts and difficulties. But these conflicts are not all bad. In fact, they are very important, because for the vast majority of Christians, marriage and family life are the divine workshop of God, where He will use just such hammerings to chisel away the rough edges of our fallen nature and make us ready for reshaping in His own image and likeness. It is the marriage relationship, and all that comes with it, that reveals our hidden flaws and forces us to deal with them, if we are to survive and to prosper spiritually, psychologically, and emotionally.

And yet, as an Orthodox priest and pastor, I have observed that even sincere, Orthodox Christians sometimes fail to recognize the potential for spiritual growth present in their daily struggles to be good husbands and wives and good parents. I think one reason for this might be that nearly all the spiritual writings from our tradition come from monastic sources. And while there is invaluable spiritual insight to be gained from them, and all Christians should avail themselves of the benefit of reading this priceless literature, still, there are aspects of married life and family life which monastic writings for the most part do not describe, simply because they occur in a different arena—the arena of marriage.

OUR COMMON CALLING

From the Scriptures and from the tradition of the Church, we know that the goal of the Christian life is growing in communion with God, often referred to as theosis or deification. And we also know that to reach this goal requires not only an absolute and unwavering trust in God, but also a certain acceptance of personal struggle and sacrifice—in a word, *asceticism*. No Orthodox Christian is exempt from this struggle, married or monastic, layperson or priest. This is common to all.

The asceticism of many of the great Orthodox monastics is well known. There are the desert-dwellers, the stylites, and the great fasters, to mention just a few. Also in the writings of the spiritual Fathers of the Church much is written about prayer and fasting, ascetical disciplines necessary for every Christian. But what about the day-to-day lives of those whom God has called to the sacrament of marriage? What ascetical opportunities are available to them?

One of the most well-known Russian saints, Seraphim of Sarov, clearly taught that the greatest ascetical duty of the monastic is not fasting or study or any other similar discipline, but rather voluntary obedience to a spiritual elder. This human interaction requires the emptying of one's own will and bending to the will of another, thereby exposing pride and dealing a death-blow to self-centeredness, the chief obstacles to spiritual growth.

I believe the same principle is involved in a marriage relationship when two people try to work together. In marriage, though, this emptying of oneself is not so much obedience to another, but rather the cooperation or coordination of two together, a dance of love and submission, the mutual losing of one's life for another. The dynamic of the monk coming before his elder, seeking spiritual guidance and direction, has its married-life counterpart in a husband and wife sitting up late into the night, working out a disagreement. The result of both should be the same—humility, repentance, unity.

If married people will see their life from this perspective, they can be inspired to embrace all their marital struggles with faith and to believe that in and through them God will reveal His will in their lives and bring about their salvation. They will not imagine that their spiritual work is something separate from their family life. They will not think that to accomplish great acts of asceticism they must look far off to the ways of monks and nuns.

Instead they will see that such opportunities are all around them, right under their very noses. They will settle down to fight the good fight where they are, and slowly, bit by bit, through the grace of God, they will be transformed to the image of His will. Let us look at some of the ascetic struggles unique to marriage and family life.

A Prayer for Married Persons

O merciful God, we beseech You always to remind us that the married state is holy, and that we must keep it so. Grant us Your grace, that we may continue in faithfulness and love. Increase in us the spirit of mutual understanding and trust, that no quarrel or strife may come between us. Grant us Your blessings, that we may stand before our fellows and in Your sight as an ideal family. And finally, by Your mercy, account us worthy of everlasting life, for You are our sanctification, and to You we ascribe glory: to the Father, and to the Son, and to the Holy Spirit, now and ever, and unto ages of ages. Amen.

THE CONTEST OF RELATIONSHIPS

Foremost is the effort necessary to build a lifelong and intimate relationship with another human being. One of the early goals of married life is for two people who possess separate backgrounds and differing personalities to form together one common vision of life, one shared understanding of their priorities and direction as a couple and as a family.

In order for this common vision to be formed, it is critical that a married couple learn to communicate, that is, to identify and express their own feelings and to listen to and understand the feelings of the other. This kind of communication requires honesty, vulnerability, courage, humility, kindness, repentance, and commitment.

Every married person soon discovers that such communication requires great effort and often emotional pain. It is a common experience for married people to discover that their spouse is like a mirror in which all of their own faults are exposed and magnified. But the humility and endurance exerted to confront these sins, to talk openly and constructively about them with one's spouse, and to use this talk to dig down and uncover the root of personal sin, can be a tremendous spiritual work.

I find that as a priest I am frequently encouraging married couples to keep up the good effort in this area and not to despair. At the same time I am saddened by those few who, for one reason or another, cannot or do not avail themselves of this most valuable aspect of their life together. I would even say that in this communication between husband and wife there is something closely akin to the cleansing and healing which take place in the sacrament of confession.

THE CONTEST OF FAMILY

The relationships involved in marriage are not limited to that between husband and wife, of course. There are also (in most cases) children, and with children come not only new sources of joy and delight, but also new opportunities for self-denial and for battling sinful passions.

Just ask the mother who for twenty years plans and prepares seven thousand sack lunches; or who, when she imagines her son fighting in a war, wrestles with sickening fear and anxiety. Ask the father who is awakened in the middle of the night by a small voice, "Daddy, I feel sick," and a moment later must deal once again with the previous evening's dinner; or who, when his son knocks over the ceramic lamp one more time, is brimming with anger and jerks back his hand to strike his child. They will tell you they see their shortcomings every day and as Christians struggle to overcome them.

Children require the very life of their parents. And as all parents know, you can, at times, actually feel this life being drained away. It is a frightening thing. Still, when it is given with love and with faith in God, the giving is a great spiritual work. The Lord said, "Greater love has no one than this, than to lay down one's life for his friends" (John 15:13). Surely these comforting words can apply to those good parents whose martyrdom is measured in tiny increments portioned out over an entire lifetime.

With children also comes the responsibility to create a family, a home where children are nurtured and where all are surrounded by love. This is one of the meanings of the crowns given to a married couple at an Orthodox wedding.

They become rulers of a small kingdom, founders, in a sense, of a small church, a place where God is worshiped and His will desired. Even this, however, cannot be an isolated kingdom, withdrawn from the rest of the world.

A family has a certain corporate responsibility, as well, to be an instrument of service and benefit to others. This is clearly expressed in one of the prayers of marriage when we pray for the new couple, "O most holy Master . . . fill their houses with bountiful food and with every good thing, so that they may give in turn to those in need."

Truly the raising of children is the most demanding call to self-denial that most adults will ever engage in throughout their lives. Oh, that our culture at large would return to such an understanding and stop the incessant beating of the drum of hedonistic self-gratification! God knows our children are suffering desperately because of it.

THE CONTEST OF STEWARDSHIP

Another area requiring ascetical effort in married life is the immense responsibility to manage property, money, and material possessions in a godly way. For married people with children, ownership of these things is not an optional luxury; it is absolutely and unequivocally required. And, again, the godly management of material goods calls for wisdom, discipline, and often self-denial.

Unfortunately, the present American culture seems obsessed with simply acquiring and consuming more and more things in an insatiable desire for greater and greater pleasure. The Christian family, therefore, must constantly struggle to turn a deaf ear to these siren calls, to mute the endless barrage of advertisements, and to live both as good stewards of what God gives them, and also as pilgrims looking for a much better world to come.

This is one reason that for a Christian family the sacrificial tithing of money to the Church is an essential, spiritual act. Perhaps you could say it is as fundamental to the Christian in the world as all-night vigils are to the monk in the monastery. It is an ascetic discipline, a

> *The physical difficulties*
> *and the emotional confrontations*
> *of marriage and family life*
> *are meant to be God's tools*
> *for "working out our salvation,"*
> *if we will let Him use them*
> *in our life.*

continual announcement to one's soul of where one's ultimate treasure truly lies.

Money is not the only resource married people and families must govern. They also must govern their time. Here again we meet with daily struggle, for certainly another terrible plague of our modern time has to be its incredible busyness. There are so many things to do, so many options before us. The problem is that few of them are inherently evil, and yet surely any one of them is potentially all-consuming.

I like to envision, therefore, that every Christian must at times pull out an imaginary machete and hack away with vengeance at all the distractions that tangle his life and threaten to choke out "the one needful thing," that is, the remembrance of God. Make no mistake here, though. Children and spouses are *not* part of that tangle to be hacked away. Rather, they are comrades in arms, as it were, those with whom and, in some ways, through whom God is bringing about our salvation.

The relationships of family, along with our regular participation in the sacramental life of the Church, provide the context in which most Christians will live out their lives. We could find no more spiritual justification for a man to flee from his family than for a monk to flee his monastery.

Still, marriage or children or family—or anything else, for that matter—must never become an idol or an end in itself. Not all marriages, even Christian ones, will succeed. Some will end in divorce, leaving behind new wounds to be healed and other struggles to be faced. And not all Christian children will remain on the spiritual path of their parents. Some will reject even parents who labored hard to do well. And there will be other struggles in store for us as well, such as aging, sickness, and death. There will be difficulties unforeseen.

But even such tragedies as these are and can be opportunities to cast ourselves into the hands of God and with ascetic struggle discover the greater depths of His indescribable grace and love. Saint Mark the Ascetic wrote, "The remembrance of God is suffering of the heart endured with a spirit of devotion." This principle of the Christian life applies equally to all, whether married or monastic. And yet, as we have seen, the forms in which it may be revealed and the framework in which it can be lived out may vary like night and day.

THE REWARDS OF DISCIPLINE

As married Christians we are called to embrace the life God has given us, and to believe He has placed all around us everything necessary for our salvation. We do not need to look far off to wish we were what we are not, or to doubt that what we have is enough. The physical difficulties and the emotional confrontations of marriage and family life are meant to be God's tools for "working out our salvation," if we will let Him use them in our life. In fact, if theosis, that is, growing in the likeness of God, is the goal of the Christian life; and if the prerequisite to this goal is the emptying of oneself of all that is sinful; then I consider that marriage can rightly be called "kenosis [emptying] for the common man."

If you are married, I exhort you to see your married life in this way, and with your mate to renew this vision throughout every stage of your life together. Commit yourself to enduring the hardships of marriage all the way from the wedding day to old age, and to learning from them. As parents, give your children the time and energy they need. Pour out your life for them, even at the expense of your own personal desires and dreams. For if you will do so, perhaps you will one day stand together beside all those you love and hear, "Well done, good and faithful servant. Enter into the joy of your Lord."

Fr. Marc Dunaway is archpriest of Saint John the Evangelist Cathedral in Eagle River, Alaska.

From AGAIN Vol. 18, No. 4.
Original publication date: December, 1995

Questions for thought and discussion:

1) Is this vision of marriage as an arena of spiritual warfare familiar to you? Do you feel prepared to embark on such a life?

2) Have you and your partner had any serious conflicts or disagreements? How can you use these to strengthen your relationship and help each other become better people?

3) Have you found it to be true that your partner is like a mirror in which all of your own faults are exposed and magnified? Think of specific ways you can openly and constructively talk with your partner about your faults, uncover the root of personal sin, and then begin to work to overcome the besetting sins in your life.

4) Do you feel your parents set a good example of self-denial and provided a secure, godly home? If not, where can you look for a model on which to build your family life?

5) Do you see your possessions and time as being on loan from God, to be used in His service? How can you cultivate this attitude?

Now that you've said "I DO"

God's Grace for Making Your Marriage Work

By Fr. Peter E. Gillquist

A bout two years ago my youngest daughter, Heidi, came up to me and said, "Daddy, I just realized something. Of all my friends at school, Courtney Shannon and I are the only two with both parents living at home."

I should not have been surprised. Kids in high school, grade school, even toddlers are coming face to face with the tragedy of marital breakdown in our society. According to the March 5, 1990, issue of *Business Week*, half of all today's marriages will end in divorce and one-fourth of all children in the U.S. live with a single parent. In many places it's becoming the exception to find both parents at home. Orthodox Christian families are not immune to this all-out assault against the institution of marriage in our day.

As Christians we say, "Something has got to be done to turn the tables around. Somehow those divorce statistics must level out, and by God's grace, start going down for a change, instead of skyrocketing higher each year." But what can we do?

THE ORTHODOX PRAYER OF MARRIAGE

There is a section in the marriage liturgy of the Orthodox Church which contains one of the most powerful prayers I've ever heard and which offers us great hope. In this prayer are four specific petitions which, if we grab hold of, understand, and trust God to answer them, will add tremendous strength and stability to our marriages. This prayer is valid not only for newly married couples hearing them pronounced at their wedding, but also for old-timers as they witness an Orthodox wedding service.

Please read this wedding prayer on page 162, and then let us examine these four petitions.

1. BLESS THEM

The first petition goes like this: "Bless them, O Lord our God, as You blessed Abraham and Sarah. Bless them, O Lord our God, as You blessed Isaac and Rebecca. Bless them, O Lord our God, as You blessed Joachim and Anna. Bless them, O Lord our God, as You blessed Zacharias and Elizabeth." The first thing we ask God for in this prayer is a blessing upon the newly married couple.

What does the word *blessing* mean? It literally means *favor.* "Favor them, O Lord." It could also mean "give them" or "bestow something good upon them." And notice the four famous couples mentioned in this petition! There is not the space available to go into detail on each couple, so let me zero in on just one pair, Isaac and Rebecca. What I have to say about these two could be amplified for all.

What tremendous drama we find in the Old Testament account of Isaac and Rebecca—one of the great "arranged marriages" of the Scriptures. Isaac needs a bride, so Abraham's servant is sent back to his homeland to find this bride. He and the Lord reach an agreement that certain things will happen so that when he meets "Miss Right," he'll know it. I encourage you to read the full story in Genesis 24.

As the account goes, the servant realizes when he sees Rebecca drawing water from a well that she must be the one. So the servant worships God and says, "Blessed be the LORD God of my master Abraham, who has not forsaken His mercy and His truth toward my master. As for me, being on the way, the LORD led me to the house of my master's brethren" (Genesis 24:27).

What did he mean by "being on the way"? He might also have said "being in the will of God," or "doing the will of God." If we obey that which we know to be true, God will lead us on to the next steps we are to take. God led the servant to Rebecca, who, in fact, was the girl He intended for Isaac.

When her family found out, they said to her, "Our sister, may you become the mother of thousands of ten thousands; and may your descendants possess the gates of those who hate them" (Genesis 24:60). Can you imagine that some families today actually *choose* to be childless! Of course their wish came true in a big way. Not only did the descendants of Rebecca and Isaac inherit the Promised Land, their descendants became the forebears of Jesus Christ.

To have your marriage blessed as God blessed the marriage of Isaac and Rebecca means that even though your coming together might not have been as dramatic, God picked you out uniquely for each other. The same blessing God gave them is upon you.

2. PRESERVE THEM

The text of this petition reads: "Preserve them, O Lord our God, as You preserved Noah in the Ark. Preserve them, O Lord our God, as You preserved the three Holy Children from the fire. And let that gladness come upon them which the blessed Helen had when she found the precious Cross."

To *preserve* means to "save," to "keep," or to "guard." God knows, our marriages today don't just need His blessing. They need His preservation! That's why the priest prays that as a man and woman come together as husband and wife, God will *preserve* their marriage.

The first of these two illustrations of preservation is a very familiar one— the story of Noah and the Ark. You remember from the Book of Genesis how there came a time not long after creation—we don't know exactly how long—when the human race turned against God. As punishment for this disobedience, God sent a great flood over the earth. But He told Noah, who was a righteous man, "Make yourself an ark of gopherwood" (Genesis 6:14).

Then God made a promise to Noah: "I will establish My covenant with you; and you shall go into the ark—you, your sons, your wife, and your sons' wives

Bless them, O Lord our God, as You blessed Abraham and Sarah.
Bless them, O Lord our God, as You blessed Isaac and Rebecca.
Bless them, O Lord our God, as You blessed Joachim and Anna.
Bless them, O Lord our God, as You blessed Zacharias and Elizabeth.

Preserve them, O Lord our God, as You preserved Noah in the Ark.
Preserve them, O Lord our God, as You preserved
the three Holy Children from the fire.
And let that gladness come upon them
which the blessed Helen had when she found the precious Cross.

Remember them, O Lord our God, as You remembered the Forty Holy Martyrs,
sending down upon them crowns from heaven.
Remember them, O Lord our God, and the parents who have nurtured them,
for the prayers of parents make firm the foundations of houses.
Remember, O Lord our God, Your servants the attendants
of the bridal pair who share in this joy.
And remember, O Lord our God,
Your servant the groom and Your handmaid the bride, and bless them.

Grant them fair children, and concord of soul and body.
Exalt them like the cedars of Lebanon,
like a luxuriant vine, that, having sufficiency in all things they may abound
in every work that is good and acceptable unto You.
And let them behold their children's children around their table,
like a newly planted olive orchard, that, obtaining favor in Your sight,
they may shine like the stars of heaven, in Thee.

with you. And of every living thing of all flesh you shall bring two of every sort into the ark, to keep them alive with you; they shall be male and female" (Genesis 6:18, 19). It rained forty days and forty nights, but Noah and those with him were preserved.

How does Noah's preservation relate to our marriages? The Ark, of course, is the Church. As a matter of fact, the main section in an Orthodox Church is known as the *nave*—an old-fashioned word for "ship" or "ark." We as persons are saved in the ark. And God preserves our marriages in the ark. We ask God to preserve our marriages in His Holy Church just as the Ark preserved Noah and his family.

The other illustration is that of the three Holy Children. I guess the story of Shadrach, Meshach, and Abed-Nego in Daniel chapter 3 has to be one of the all-time favorite miracles in the entire Bible. I remember as a young person listening enthralled about the evil King Nebuchadnezzar who decided he would erect an idol and command everybody to worship it. Daniel was the dedicated young prophet who had three buddies named Shadrach, Meshach, and Abed-Nego.

The king said, "Whoever does not fall down and worship shall be cast immediately into the midst of a burning fiery furnace" (v. 6). Daniel's three friends declined the invitation. When they were brought before the king, he asked them, "Is it true, Shadrach, Meshach, and Abed-Nego, that you do not serve my gods or worship the gold image which I have set up?" (v. 14). He threatened them with the furnace.

Their response was a classic: "O Nebuchadnezzar, we have no need to answer you in this matter. If that is the case, our God whom we serve is able to deliver us from the burning fiery furnace, and He will deliver us from your hand, O king. But if not, let it be known to you, O king, that we do not serve your gods, nor will we worship the gold image which you have set up" (vv. 16-18).

Let me ask, are you going through fiery trials in your marriage? Listen, God is able to preserve you as He preserved these three young men. That is why we pray, "Preserve them, O Lord our God, as You preserved the three Holy Children from the fire." Nebuchadnezzar was so enraged at these three unbending teenagers, he told his servants to stoke the furnace up seven times hotter than usual. It was so hot that the guys who had to throw Shadrach, Meshach, and Abed-Nego into the flames were themselves burned to a crisp right on the spot.

But what about the three young men? Scripture states that not only were they preserved, not a hair on their bodies was singed. The king looked over the edge of the furnace and was flabbergasted. "Did we not cast three men bound into the midst of the fire?" he asked. "I see four men loose, walking in the midst of the fire; and they are not hurt, and the form of the fourth is like the Son of God" (vv. 24, 25). Our Lord Jesus Christ, the Son of God and second Person of the Trinity, joined them in the fire!

Do you know that Christ joins you, even when your marriage heats up? That's why this prayer is in the wedding service! Christ is not only the head of the Church, and the Lord of our lives, but He is also in charge of our homes. It

is in Him that the peace and unity of marriage is secure. So we ask God to preserve the newly married couple as He preserved the three Holy Children in the scorching flames. Nebuchadnezzar was so impressed with what he saw that he started praising God and threatened dire consequences to anyone who harmed Shadrach, Meshach, and Abed-Nego.

Where do we find safety for our marriages? In the hands of Christ and His Church. You can't get any safer than that. If you have a problem in your marriage, bring it to your priest. There is no shame in having problems. I'd venture to say all of us, to one degree or another, have experienced problems. The shame is in hiding your problems. The devil loves to creep in and force a wedge between you and your mate. He can be defeated though, just as Nebuchadnezzar was defeated, if we bring our problems to Jesus Christ in His Church.

3. REMEMBER THEM

In the third petition of the marriage prayer, we find these words: "Remember them, O Lord our God, as You remembered the Forty Holy Martyrs, sending down upon them crowns from heaven. Remember them, O Lord our God, and the parents who have nurtured them, for the prayers of the parents make firm the foundations of houses."

The illustration here is, I think, one of the most fantastic stories of the saints in all of history. It was March in the year 320. There was an emperor named Lycinius who at one time had favored the Christians, but for political reasons changed his mind. Lycinius set up a decree in Cappadocia, ordering every Christian on pain of death to abandon his or her faith in Christ.

When the governor of Cappadocia and Armenia communicated this decree to the army, forty young soldiers immediately stepped forward, refusing to worship idols or to deny Christ. These forty men of various nationalities were stationed at a place called Sebaste, which is in modern-day Turkey. They all belonged to the famous Thundering Legion—an elite, combat-ready squadron of their day.

The faithful soldiers were called to appear at a tribunal where they announced that no torment would ever induce them to give up their Christian faith. The governor first tried persuasive compromise, which got him nowhere. Next, he turned to more deadly tactics. He ordered them to be tortured and thrown into prison. Their reply was to start singing together Psalm 91: "He who dwells in the secret place of the Most High shall abide under the shadow of the Almighty." What a great song for men preparing to meet their Maker in the face of persecution.

The governor was out of control over their continued steadfastness, and decided to subject them to a very strange ordeal. March is said to be the coldest month in Sebaste. The whole area was frozen over, including the lake just next to the gates of the city. The governor ordered the forty men to be stripped down and made to stand out on the frozen lake naked until they either renounced Christ or froze to death.

Eager to serve the Lord, they didn't wait for the guards to strip them of their clothes. They undressed themselves and stepped out on the ice, saying that it was an honor to die for Jesus Christ. Tradition tells us that some of these men lasted three days and nights. Together they prayed, "We are forty who are engaged in this conflict. Grant that forty may be crowned and that we may not fall short of that sacred number."

During all of this, the guards were continually urging them to offer up sacrifices to the false gods so that they could move near the inviting warm fire they had built for them on the shore. Finally, one of their number recanted. He walked to the bonfire, only to perish from the sudden heat on his frozen body.

But one of the guards was so struck by the courage of the thirty-nine men that he flung off his clothes, stepped out onto the ice, and took his place among the tortured, proclaiming himself to be a Christian. By his martyrdom, he obtained the grace and the martyr's crown which had been forfeited by the one who deserted. God had indeed heard the prayer of the soldiers and answered it in this wholly unexpected way. So the new convert got the fortieth crown and the Church received one of her most striking examples of faith, martyrdom, and courage.

Now, listen to that prayer again. "Remember them, O Lord our God, as You remembered the Forty Holy Martyrs." God did not desert them out there, but He sent His angelic hosts to robe and crown them in their death. He even filled up the one spot left vacant. That's how God will remember you in your marriage. Keep on obeying Him no matter what! Let me tell you something. God will never forget you or abandon you as a married couple. As He looks down upon your marriage, He sees you and exalts you as He crowned those forty heroic soldiers there at Sebaste.

There is one other "remember" I want to mention in this prayer: "Remember them, O Lord our God, and the parents who have nurtured them"—and hear this, parents, "for the prayers of parents make firm the foundations of houses." Most likely, the prayers of your parents helped you to be where you are today. That is why the Book of Proverbs says, "Train up a child in the way he should go, and when he is old he will not depart from it" (Proverbs 22:6). Parents, don't ever stop praying for your children!

4. GRANT THEM

The final petition says: "Grant them fair children and concord of soul and body." In this sick age of abortion on demand, I want to remind you that one of the greatest things God can do for your marriage is to send along children. I can't put into words what children do for a marriage. The abundance of children in a home is a blessed gift from God.

And then the part I like best about this prayer: "And let them behold their children's children around their table like a newly planted olive orchard, that, obtaining favor in Your sight, they may shine like the stars of heaven, in Thee."

I'll tell you, as wonderful as it is to have children, the fulfillment of having children is having grandchildren! Parents, you are always parents. You are never through being moms and dads, even when the kids leave home. Things change, because they are off on their own, establishing their own families and their lives, but nonetheless, moms and dads are always moms and dads, right on into eternity. My dad is in his eighties, and when I go home he's still Dad and I'm still his son. Even though I'm a father and a grandfather, when I'm at his house, I'm still a son. Our job as parents does not end the day our children walk the aisle as man and wife. The next phase of *parenthood* is *grandparenthood,* and the joy of beholding your children's children.

Well, how's that for stability in Orthodox marriage? First, God *blesses us* as He blessed the patriarchs. All the blessings that He gave to Isaac and Rebecca and the rest of the patriarchal couples are given us as we are joined in Christ to each other. Next, God *preserves* our marriages just the way he preserved Noah and his family from the flood and the three Holy Children from the fire. God also *remembers us* as He remembered those forty martyrs. That same grace is there for us. And finally, He *grants us* children and grandchildren to enrich our lives with joy and favor.

If you are faithful to the Lord, your marriage will be one of His stunning trophies of grace for all eternity.

Fr. Peter E. Gillquist
Publisher, AGAIN Magazine

From AGAIN Vol. 13, No. 2.
Original publication date: June, 1990

Questions for thought and discussion:

God's grace is abundantly given in the marriage ceremony, but it is up to you as a couple to receive and preserve that grace. What do you need to do to preserve the grace of being:

1) blessed like Isaac and Rebecca?

2) preserved like Noah and the three Holy Children?

3) remembered like the Forty Holy Martyrs?

4) granted children and grandchildren?

CROWN
THEM
WITH
& GLORY
HONOR

By Fr. David Anderson

Breathtakingly beautiful to behold, the Orthodox marriage liturgy is filled from start to finish with scriptural symbolism and mystery. As an Orthodox priest, I have had the privilege of officiating at dozens of these services over the past years. Often I have found myself compelled to explain what was going to take place, or what did take place during the course of the wedding service, for most Americans are unaccustomed to the Orthodox marriage tradition. I find that a degree of confusion also exists among Orthodox Christians concerning various aspects of this beautiful liturgy.

Of course there are many similarities between Orthodox weddings and the weddings traditional to our Western culture. Familiar elements exist: A beautiful church resplendent with flowers.

Elegantly dressed men and women. A beautifully adorned bride and a nervous bridegroom. An officiant or officiants. The list goes on.

But there are also some important differences. To clarify some of the confusion which exists on both sides, I want to walk through the Orthodox wedding liturgy step by step with you, to give a basic understanding of what is happening and why.

DEVELOPMENT OF THE WEDDING LITURGY

It is not possible to understand an Orthodox wedding service without a brief historical frame of reference. All of the Church's services have undergone a long historical development. This is especially true of the marriage service.

In the early centuries, there was no

special liturgy of marriage, as we have now. Both in the Roman Empire, and for a long time in the Byzantine Empire, marriage was understood as a civil or legal contract. All of the modern Western marriage services, which focus on the exchange of vows, reflect this legal inheritance. During the Roman and Byzantine periods, a Christian man and woman would go to the appropriate imperial agency for the marriage contract to be signed. Their marriage in Christ, as members of the Church, was sealed later, when they received Communion together at the liturgy, and were blessed by the bishop.

In time, the Church "took over" from the state the entire process of the marriage, and thus the present liturgy of marriage consists of two parts: the betrothal and the crowning. The service of the betrothal, which, according to historical practice, takes place in the vestibule or narthex of the church, is the equivalent of the "natural" or "civil" marriage.

But a "civil" marriage alone is not enough for those who have died to this world and whose lives are hidden with Christ in God. Once the betrothal, the earthly marriage, has been completed in the narthex, the priest leads the bridal pair into the church, into the Kingdom of God, where the water of their earthly union will be transformed into the wine of that union which is the same as the mystery of Christ and the Church (Ephesians 5:32).

HEAVENLY PROCESSIONS

The two parts of the marriage service are joined by a procession into the Church. This procession follows the same pattern established by the Church for baptisms and the Eucharist. At baptism, it is the entrance of the newly baptized and chrismated, clothed in their white garments, having died in the font

to this world of death and sin, which provides the visual liturgical focus of the Christian life as a procession, a passover, from death to life, from earth to heaven.

Likewise, at the Divine Liturgy, a series of processional movements reveals the essential experience of the Christian life. Our earthly life is a passage out of this world to God's Table in His Kingdom. The members of the Church assemble to become one body, just as the many grains of wheat together form one bread. The Word of God in the Gospels leads the clergy to the altar. The bread and wine, symbol of our lives, are carried to the altar, and then are lifted on high. The Church advances to receive Communion.

In the same way, the tradition of the Church gave birth to the liturgy of marriage within this paschal, baptismal, and eucharistic framework. Just as the earthly bread and wine move forward to become the Body and Blood of the Lord, so the man and woman, betrothed in this world, move forward to become the icon of Christ and the Church.

THE BETROTHAL

As we have said, the first part of the marriage, the betrothal, appropriately takes place at the entrance of the Church. The groom and bride arrive with their attendants to freely offer themselves to each other. According to Western practice, the bride enters the church, accompanied by her father or another male figure, to be "given away" before the altar. This custom runs counter to the traditional Orthodox understanding. In Orthodox marriages, the bride and groom are united at the entrance of the church. Their entry together into the church is a movement from the natural union to the ultimate mystery of union in Christ.

The betrothal consists of an opening blessing by the priest, followed by a special litany in which the Church asks God to bless the marriage with those things most needed: salvation (always the first and greatest need), perfect and peaceful love, oneness of mind, steadfastness of faith, the procreation of children, blamelessness and fidelity. The priest concludes this litany with a prayer addressed to God "who has brought together into unity the things which before had been separate, and has ordained for them an indissoluble bond of love."

Thus at the very beginning of the marriage union we see reflections of a much larger reality—that of the salvation of the human race. Just as God and man, who had become separated, are united in Christ, so also in Christ human beings, separated by sin and selfishness, can be reconciled in an indissoluble bond of love.

The priest then prays another prayer: "O Lord our God, who espoused the Church as a pure virgin from the Gentiles, bless this betrothal, and unite these Your servants, keeping them in peace and oneness of mind." The same love which made God the Bridegroom of Israel in the Old Covenant, and which unites Christ to His Bride the Church, is called upon to unite the man and woman.

The sign of the betrothal, the rings, are then blessed and exchanged three times, in the Name of the Holy Trinity. The priest then says a long prayer, in which the creation of the human race as men and women is praised as an act of divine providence, and the biblical history of the ring as a symbol of fidelity is reviewed. The betrothed couple are then ready for their entrance into the church.

THE CROWNING

The second part of the wedding, the marriage proper, most often called the crowning, begins with a glorious procession in which the priest, as Christ, leads the man and woman to the front of the

As jeweled or floral crowns are placed upon the heads of the bride and groom, the priest exclaims, "O Lord our God, crown them with glory and honor!" The wedding crowns have a double meaning rooted in Scripture: they are the signs both of royalty and of martyrdom.

church, while he chants the marriage psalm, Psalm 128: "Blessed is everyone who fears the Lord, who walks in His ways! You shall eat the fruit of the labor of your hands; you shall be happy, and it shall be well with you. Your wife shall be as a fruitful vine within your house; your children like olive branches around your table. . . The Lord bless you from Zion! May you see the good things of Jerusalem all the days of your life. . ." The people respond, singing in a triumphant melody, "Glory to You, Our God, glory to You!" after each verse.

The couple are then presented with lighted candles, reminiscent of baptism and Pascha, and the priest declares the "destination" of the liturgy with the eucharistic blessing: "Blessed is the Kingdom of the Father, and of the Son, and of the Holy Spirit. . ." A litany follows, asking for the Lord to be present as He was in Cana, to grant salvation, children, blamelessness, and gladness.

The priest then says the three great prayers of marriage. These are prayers of thanksgiving. Through these prayers, what marriage *is* is revealed. God is praised for revealing the union of man and woman as the source of blessing: the great promise of the Old Covenant, that through the offspring of Abraham all peoples would be blessed, has been fulfilled through that human love which united Abraham and Sarah, Isaac and Rebecca, Jacob and Rachel, Joseph and Asenath, Moses and Zipporah, and reached its climax in the unions of Zechariah and Elizabeth, from whom John the Baptist, the ultimate prophet, was born, and of Joachim and Anna, from whom came forth the Virgin Mary, the Mother of God, whose virgin birth of God in the flesh ushers in the new creation.

It is God Himself who is the "holy Celebrant of mystical and pure marriage." In these prayers, His Church asks Him to pour the riches of all the blessing He has shown from the beginning of time upon the marriage now taking place.

Next, as the sign of this union of man and woman being transformed into a divine union in Christ, the bride and groom are crowned in the name of the Father, the Son, and the Holy Spirit. As jeweled or floral crowns are placed upon the heads of the bride and groom, the priest exclaims, "O Lord our God, crown them with glory and honor!"

The wedding crowns have a double meaning rooted in Scripture: they are the signs both of royalty and of martyrdom. In Christ, fallen human beings who have lost their royal dignity, trapped in a web of death and sin, are restored and re-created as kings and queens of the new creation. But this restoration depends on the Cross, and the Cross means far more than accepting that "Jesus did it for me." The Cross means being crucified with Christ in this world, and the death of the self-centered pride so deeply rooted within our fallen hearts.

The Church is saying to the newly married couple: "You have been united as fallen human beings, but Christ has made you a king and a queen. For the rest of your life you must become what He has begun to make you. Your love must be His sacrificial love, and your life together must be a martyrdom, a crucifixion. Christ was glorified in His crucifixion, and His martyrs were exalted through suffering and death. This is the royal way of love."

THE READINGS FROM SCRIPTURE

At this point in the marriage liturgy, two passages of Scripture are read before the couple and in the presence of the entire Church.

The reading from the Epistle to the Ephesians describes the marriage union as the image of the union between Christ and the Church. "[Submit] to one another in the fear of God. Wives, submit to your own husbands, as to the Lord. . . . Just as the church is subject to Christ, so let the wives be to their own husbands in everything. Husbands, love your wives, just as Christ also loved the church and gave Himself for her" (Ephesians 5:21-25).

Submission means mutual sacrifice. Christ revealed His headship not through any demonstration of what the world understands as masculine power, but by washing the feet of His Apostles (who were being very "masculine"—quarrelling about who was the greatest), and then going to His voluntary death. It is to this revelation of true masculinity that the Church submits herself as a bride, and Saint Paul's words must be understood in this context.

The Gospel reading of Christ's first miracle at the wedding in Cana (John chapter 2) tells of the transformation of water into wine. This is the image of the Christian life, and of Christian marriage.

By His grace, through His mercy and love, the water of our lives can be transformed into unspeakable glory. "Beloved, now we are children of God; and it has not yet been revealed what we shall be, but we know that when He is revealed, we shall be like Him" (1 John 3:2).

THE CUP OF BLESSING AND THE DANCE OF JOY

At this point in the present marriage service, a cup of wine is blessed and shared by the newly married couple. Originally, the wedding continued and reached its climax in the celebration of the Eucharist. For it is at the Lord's Table that His people eat and become His Body in this world, and the reception of Holy Communion should be the first act of marriage. Hopefully the desire for the renewal of the liturgy shared by many Orthodox will result in our time in the restoration of the Eucharist to the sacrament of marriage.

The final act of the service consists of another procession: the priest, holding the Cross, leads the couple three times around a table placed at the front of the Church, while hymns to the Virgin Mary and the martyrs are sung: "Rejoice, O Isaiah! A Virgin is with child; and shall bear a Son, Emmanuel. He is both God and man; and Orient is His name. Magnifying Him, we call the Virgin Blessed." This circular procession, a solemn "dance of joy," is an image of life in Christ: the Cross leads us, the Gospel on the table is our sun, and we revolve around it. The obedience of the Mother of God and the martyrs' faithfulness unto death are our models.

Following this procession, the bridal crowns are removed, and the priest prays that the Lord will "receive their crowns into [His] Kingdom." What has been made visible through the liturgy will now continue invisibly as we pass through life

The liturgy of marriage condenses everything that has been experienced by God's people about married life in Christ into a wine as new and strong as that made by Christ in Cana of Galilee.

in this world, with our true life hidden with Christ in God, as we strive in faith for the good work He has begun in us to be brought to perfection.

A QUIET MIRACLE

This, in very rudimentary form, is what takes place at every Orthodox wedding. The liturgy has developed over the course of centuries, yet hearkens back to the early days of the Church, when the entire service was celebrated in the context of the Eucharist on Sunday morning.

I would be remiss in not mentioning one last element which exists at Orthodox weddings. One might call this final element the "miraculous" element.

In the fullest meaning of the word, a miracle occurs whenever the members of the Body of Christ assemble to visibly become the Church—to become together what they cannot become as isolated individuals. This miracle is nearly always (there are exceptions!) a quiet, invisible miracle: a miracle that goes unnoticed by this world, a miracle that cannot be seen without the "eyesight of the Kingdom." In this miracle, the merely chronological time of this world is transcended and the time of

God's eternal "present tense" is revealed. The Kingdom of God is made manifest, not as something to be revealed in a future setting, but as a present reality.

This miraculous element is uniquely evident in the Orthodox liturgy of marriage. The liturgy of marriage is not simply a beautiful and meaningful service. It cannot be reduced to words or concepts—it is not just a declaration of everything the Church believes about marriage. Rather, the liturgy of marriage *is* marriage, just as the liturgy of baptism *is* baptism, or the liturgy of the Eucharist *is* offering and communion.

When the Church assembles to be the Church, God becomes present. The liturgy of marriage condenses everything that has been experienced by God's people about married life in Christ into a wine as new and strong as that made by Christ in Cana of Galilee. As Christ was present at that wedding to perform His first miracle, so He is present at each new wedding. Miraculously, the temporal is transformed into the eternal as a man and woman are joined in the sacrament of Holy Marriage.

Fr. David Anderson serves as priest of Saints Peter and Paul Church in Ben Lomond, California.

From AGAIN Vol. 13, No. 2.
Original publication date: June, 1980

Questions for thought and discussion:

1) Walk through the wedding service point by point. Refer to the full text of the wedding liturgy from a service book, as well as the explanations given in this article. Discuss together the meaning of each of the prayers and actions of the liturgy.

a) What is being promised during the betrothal? What is the meaning of the exchange of rings?

b) What is the significance of the procession to the front of the church after the betrothal? Reflect on the words of Psalm 128.

c) What do the wedding crowns signify?

d) When you hear the epistle reading, what is its message to you personally? What does the Gospel reading say to you?

e) What is the significance of the cup of blessing? How is this different from the eucharistic cup?

f) What is the meaning of the circular procession or "dance of joy"?

g) What is the significance of the removal of the crowns?

2) "When the Church assembles to be the Church, God becomes present. . . . As Christ was present at that wedding to perform His first miracle, so He is present at each new wedding." How does knowing that Christ will be present at your wedding affect your view of marriage and your attitude about the upcoming ceremony itself?

PLAIN
TALK on
MARRIAGE

by Fr. Gordon Thomas Walker

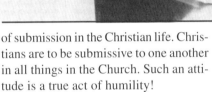

O f all the services I have had the joy to celebrate as an Orthodox priest, the wedding ceremony is truly among the most beautiful. An Orthodox wedding is totally sacramental from start to finish. The wedding garments are sacramental. The service is sacramental. Even the marriage feast afterward is a sacramental act.

The beauty of the wedding ceremony goes far beyond the service itself. We are drawn to the righteousness of the saints, and to the Church triumphant as she is presented to Christ on the final Day. As a sacramental union, marriage is intended by God to be a recipient of grace continually flowing, first to the new family and then out into the surrounding world.

In our age of skyrocketing divorce rates, Christian couples need to work doubly hard at making their marriages shine. They are called to do more than just stay together. Christian marriages are meant to show forth something of heaven on earth, and to display the presence of Christ with His Church. True marriage is highly evangelical in nature, proclaiming the beauty of our union with Christ. Therefore, wanting a good marriage and working toward it is not selfish.

ADVICE TO CHRISTIAN WOMEN

Ephesians chapter 5 is the epistle read at the Orthodox wedding service. In it Saint Paul teaches the importance of submission in the Christian life. Christians are to be submissive to one another in all things in the Church. Such an attitude is a true act of humility!

In verse 22 of this chapter, the Apostle writes, "Wives, submit to your own husbands, as to the Lord." Here, Christian submission is shown to be the specific role of the wife. Modern femi nists have twisted the meaning of this passage in an apparent effort to make submission of a wife to her husband an unpopular topic in our day and age. But far from demeaning the rights and value of women, this passage actually bestows the highest possible honor upon the married Christian woman. In submitting to her husband, she becomes an image of the Church, which is in submission to Christ! Ultimately she is an image of Christ Himself, who is in complete submission to the will of His Father. Anyone care to disparage that honor?

Submission has nothing whatever to do with equality or non-equality before God. It has everything to do with the *roles* we are called upon to take in this great drama of salvation. The husband is to image the Lord as head of the family, and the wife is to respect his headship. Thus, the Christian family becomes an icon of the Holy Trinity.

Is it always easy for a wife to submit to her husband? No one could ever make such a claim. But if you as a wife accept this role and practice it, God will bless you for it. Being submissive simply means accepting your husband as the God-appointed head of the home. I believe women need to work at giving their husbands opportunities to exercise authority and also work at being submissive to their headship, showing them honor. In doing this, a wife will bring out the best in her husband and in turn receive the best from him.

ADVICE TO CHRISTIAN MEN

For men, the Apostle's command is even tougher. For love is the next instruction given by Saint Paul. "Husbands, you have the greater responsibility of loving your wives as Christ loved the Church." It is the role of a husband to love his wife unselfishly, even to the extent of being willing to die if need be for his mate. But if you as a husband will accept that role and give yourself to it, God will bless and strengthen you for it.

Without a doubt, 1 Corinthians 13 is the most beautiful description of love ever written. When you think about the countless words written about love throughout the history of humanity, it is incredible that such a short passage could so perfectly summarize love:

Though I speak with the tongues of men and of angels, but have not love, I have become as sounding brass or a clanging cymbal. And though I have the gift of prophecy, and understand all mysteries and all knowledge, and though I have all faith, so that I could remove mountains, but have not love, I am nothing. And though I bestow all my goods to feed the poor, and though I give my body to be burned, but have not love, it profits me nothing. Love suffers long and is kind; love does not envy; love does not parade itself, is not puffed up; does not behave rudely, does not seek its own, is not provoked, thinks no evil; does not rejoice in iniquity, but rejoices in the truth; bears all things, believes all things, hopes all things, endures all things. Love never fails.

This is the kind of love the husband is to initiate. What a tall order! In doing so he follows the role of the Heavenly Father, who is the Fountainhead of the Trinity. As the wife submits herself to her husband, she mirrors the relationship between God the Son and God the Father. As the husband seeks to pattern himself after the Heavenly Father, he becomes the initiator of love in the family.

HUSBANDS AS SUCCESSFUL LOVERS

This sacrificial love of the husband for the wife is a crucial ingredient of any marriage. For the husband to become a successful lover, at least two things are necessary.

1) The husband must become a giver

Instead of always taking, the husband must learn to give himself and his love away. Certainly it is all right for husbands to receive love that has been given to them. In fact, husbands and wives *need* to be receivers of their spouses' love. To reject love that has been extended is a crushing insult. We need to learn how to receive love as well as to give it. But husbands must first become givers of love and then learn how to be receivers of love.

2) The husband must become a *for*giver

If the husband carries around a little black notebook with the record of every time his spouse has injured him, including every negative word that's been said, or all the episodes that may have happened days or weeks or months or years ago, he will never be a lover. He will always be into self-preservation.

It seems strange, but often we can forgive almost anybody but our mates. It happens all the time. We will be patient and understanding and forgiving of others outside the home, but harsh and demanding and unforgiving within it. Husbands, it's up to us to turn this around. We must set the example and be the initiators of love and forgiveness, and see if it doesn't come back to us.

ADVICE TO PARENTS

Another area in which husbands and wives must follow the example set by God the Father in His heavenly family is the teaching and training of children. Saint Paul says in verse 1 of Ephesians chapter 6, "Children, obey your parents in the Lord, for this is right." Obviously it is up to parents to set godly standards of discipline so that their children can be obedient to the Lord. Of the many things children must learn, at least two are basic.

1) Love

You must love them and let them know it. Tell them often, "I love you." And by all means back up these words with acts of love. It is also very important for a husband and wife to demonstrate love to each other for the well-being of their children. Doing this provides the security that they need. They need to know mother and dad love each other. It is important to hug and kiss each other, to hold hands in front of your kids. They need to see open expressions of affection from time to time. We must not be phony about it, but genuinely show love to each other.

2) Obedience

The best time to start teaching obedience? As early as you can! As soon as the child starts exhibiting rebellious tendencies, you must start teaching him or her obedience. Do so gently at first, but do it persistently, faithfully, and firmly.

Some post-modern psychologists insist we should not use physical punishment. Not only has their misguided advice helped to produce an undisciplined generation of school children, their counsel is in direct disagreement with God's instructions on the matter. Listen to Proverbs 13:24: "He who spares his rod hates his son, but he who loves him disciplines him promptly [or early]." This means early in life. You don't wait until a child becomes set in his attitudes and rebellious in his ways, and then try to use the rod. Most children will learn obedience and respect for authority best if we use the "rod" judiciously. (I personally recommend a paint paddle. They are flimsy and won't bruise, but make a nice attention-getting smack.)

Children need to know where the boundaries are, and it's usually the father's responsibility to initiate discipline as well as love in the family. That doesn't mean that the mother can't discipline when the father is away. But generally speaking, it is Dad's duty to set the parameters and patterns of discipline, and to be faithful and work hard at teaching and training children early in life.

By the way, in Ephesians 6:4, Saint Paul cautions fathers to use corrective

> O God, our God,
>
> who did come to Cana of Galilee,
>
> and did bless there the marriage feast:
>
> bless also these Your servants,
>
> who through Your good providence
>
> are now united together in wedlock . . .
>
> Receive their crowns into Your Kingdom,
>
> preserving them spotless, blameless,
>
> and without reproach.

A prayer from the Orthodox wedding liturgy

measures carefully. "Do not provoke your children to wrath, but bring them up in the training and admonition [or discipline] of the Lord." Sometimes fathers can be too harsh and provoke their children to bitterness and anger. We fathers must remember to discipline in love. Be firm and clear, but also loving. Our goal is to mold our children toward love, loyalty, and obedience—not wrath. And this is particularly crucial for us to remember as they get older. As children mature, they will want to know the reasons *why* you tell them to do some things and not to do others. We need to have our answers ready.

The raising of children is never something we can consider finished or accomplished. After you have raised your own children, and they get married and start having their children, then you have adult offspring to be concerned about and pray for. Sometimes adult offspring will come to you for help more than they ever have before! It seems we are never finished. We have to keep at it. I find myself constantly burning candles for my children and grandchildren, praying earnestly for them.

A HEAVENLY MARRIAGE REQUIRES EARTHLY WORK

If you expect your marriage to be a heavenly one, you must *work* at making it so. And I *do* mean work. My wife and I have worked at this business of being married for going on four decades, trying to do the things that we knew were best for our marriage.

For one thing, you must work at *communicating*. Communicating is not easy. Don't just assume that you are doing a good job of communicating, and don't put all the responsibility and burden on your mate. You must be willing to go more than fifty percent to be a good communicator. If both of you are willing to do so, it will balance out.

We recommend a book designed to help with the art of communicating, *Ten Weeks to a Better Marriage.* I have found, as Mary Sue and I have conducted marriage seminars, that often husbands and wives are shocked at the things that come out as they begin to communicate. They discover feelings they have never known about or discussed. I have heard husbands and wives say, "If I had known that, I would have done things differently." They didn't know because the work of communicating had not been done.

One of the most beautiful things about an Orthodox wedding is the crowning ceremony. The crowns represent not only the victory that comes through love in marriage but also the martyr's crown. There is a martyrdom in marriage. You must be willing to die to yourself, to your own little ways of doing things. You will find you must give in to your mate at many points along the way. Both of you will. But the Scriptures teach that if we accept the crown of martyrdom without resisting it, resenting it, or rebelling against it, out of that will come great joy. Our joy will become increasingly full as we accept the martyrdom required to make our marriages work.

A MARRIAGE MADE IN HEAVEN

The Orthodox Church views marriage as eternal. If you have been only *partially* successful in making your marriage a heavenly one, you will find joy in the fact that it is forever. You've got some time to bring it up to speed! If you really want your marriage to reflect that heavenly dimension, and you are willing to work at it, you will see a change take place. It may not happen instanta-

neously. The rate at which ice melts depends on how big the block of ice is that you're trying to thaw out. Maybe your marriage problems have become the size of a glacial iceberg that needs to be melted down. Be patient. Give God time. Let Him work with you, and let Him work with your mate. Work at making your marriage better.

True Christian marriages are made in heaven, but they must be made to work on earth. Christian couple, whether you are just starting out on a brand new life together, or looking back on years of married bliss, pledge today to commit or recommit yourselves and your marriage to God. It's worth everything you have to offer, and a whole lot more. Let's work together with God to make our marriages and our homes an icon of heaven here on earth.

Fr. Gordon Thomas Walker
St. Ignatius Orthodox Church
Franklin, Tennessee

From AGAIN Vol. 13, No. 2.
Original publication date: June, 1990

Questions for thought and discussion:

1) How do you understand the concept of submission?

2) Compare your love for your partner to that described in 1 Corinthians 13. What areas do you need to work on?

3) Are you comfortable with both giving love and receiving love?

4) Did you feel loved by your parents? Do you feel you will know how to demonstrate love to your children?

5) How does each of you view discipline of children? What behavior do you consider acceptable or unacceptable? What methods of discipline are you comfortable with?

FIVE SECRETS OF A HAPPY MARRIAGE

BY FR. GORDON THOMAS AND MARY SUE WALKER

Y̲ou know you're getting old when a magazine editor calls and asks you to look back over the years and share your secrets of a happy marriage with "young and middle-aged readers"! June 5, 1987 will mark our thirty-fifth year (by the time this book goes to press, we will have been married for over forty-three years!).

Together we've identified the five ingredients we feel were pivotal in making those years of union together in Christ ones of joy and security—even in the tougher times. In gratitude to the Lord, let us share those secrets with you.

SECRET #1: LEARN TO VERBALIZE YOUR LOVE

A love-filled marriage is not automatic. Instead, it requires that we constantly work at staying in love and making our love grow. Remember, marriage is the soil in which love grows—it is not the love itself. And as in any living thing, we must carefully cultivate that love in order to make it grow. Three phrases have helped us cultivate a growing marriage.

"Forgive Me"

The hardest words you will ever say to your spouse are, "I was wrong, please forgive me." If you can't bring yourself to say "forgive me," at least say "I'm sorry"!

GORDON: I must confess my wife has been more faithful at this than I. But I believe a most important practice of our marriage has been coming to one another and apologizing when we have wronged each other.

Asking forgiveness is a mark of true spirituality. Do it in your marriage. Don't debate with yourself about it! Use the hard words "forgive me" and when you do, you will find yourself growing in sensitivity. You will begin to think twice before you blurt out harsh and unloving remarks, or do the things you know will hurt your mate.

"Thank You"

MARY SUE: Being grateful is another hallmark of a true Christian. Wives, when your husband opens the door for you—as he faithfully did when you were courting—don't forget to smile and say "thank you" (after you've come out of your state of shock!)

GORDON: And husbands, if your wife cooks your favorite dish, be sure to say "thank you." One of my fond childhood memories is that of my father often saying after a meal, "I enjoyed the meal, Mrs. Walker."

IT IS THE *ESSENCE* OF TRUE MANHOOD TO BECOME RESPONSIBLE AND COMMUNICATE LOVE.

"I Love You"

"I love you." No one ever tires of hearing those words. And as you say them or write them (love notes to your spouse are a valuable aid to staying in love), you will find your love growing.

GORDON: Don't be like the Englishman who said to his wife, "I told you I loved you the day we married, and if things should change, I'll let you know." Men are often guilty of being unexpressive about love. They feel clumsy and easily embarrassed or perhaps even unmanly in saying "I love you." It is the *essence* of true manhood to become responsible and communicate love. Say the words frequently—both to start out the day and before going to sleep.

MARY SUE: Even without a lot of premarital advice, I knew that continu-ing to say "I love you" after a marriage was extremely important. Father Gordon is very verbal with his love (I have figured out even with his traveling he must have told me he loves me over 21,000 times. That's 35 years x 300 days x 2!)

You would think that would be enough, and I would believe him. But we live in the present, and I must hear it every day or I assume something is wrong. If we have a disagreement, misunderstanding, or if I get my feelings hurt, it is even more important that I hear it—as well as say it.

SECRET #2: MAKE MEALTIMES A SACRAMENT

MARY SUE: My mom always cooked a big meal at night, and we all sat down and ate together as a family. Father Gordon's parents did the same. It was natural that as newlyweds, we followed their practice. Although we didn't understand sacrament then, we did know that God blessed us as the family was together around the table. Over the years we have made it a priority to be home at mealtimes whenever possible.

GORDON: My warmest childhood memory is of our dinner times together. My mother would have dinner ready when my dad came home from work. We would all sit down together, but no one served himself or took a bite until Dad prayed. Then we ate and listened as he told what had gone on at the shop and Mother told about her day's events. The kids always chimed in with their experiences and comments. Those warm memories have greatly shaped my own paternal habits.

It requires sacrifice for mothers to prepare good food and serve it well, especially when they work outside the home. But that sacrifice will pay great dividends. Mothers hold the key for making mealtimes a success.

Perhaps the husband's greatest responsibility—and the easiest to neglect—is to take the lead in family Bible reading and prayers. At our house, this usually took place at breakfast. I simply read through books of the Bible a few verses at a time.

When children are small, stop in the middle of verses and ask simple questions. Our children would often "zone out" when I was reading, so the questions helped them to pay attention. Once when I had only read half a verse and asked a question, our daughter Melissa looked up with her big brown eyes and replied, "I can't *be member,* Daddy." Children have a short attention span, I kept telling myself! But nothing is more helpful to family stability than regular Bible reading and prayers together.

SECRET #3: FIGHT FOR FAMILY TIME

GORDON: All of us feel the pressures of a very busy life. I find I must schedule time for Mary Sue and me to be together. We especially enjoy going out for dinner, or taking two or three days in the Smoky Mountains. But honestly, we are not a good example in this respect. Most couples need more time together than we set aside. The strength of our marriage in other areas helps overcome our lack of private time.

As for family time, we have also struggled for this through the years. We have taken trips together—and even gone on picnics in the rain eating under a gazebo rather than cancel the family outing. When I schedule an event, I find I often fight to keep it from folding. We have taken all our children with us on trips at rather heavy financial sacrifice, rather than leave them home. I once drove most of the night in order to attend my son's basketball game. Mary Sue has frequently given up other plans to take one of the children to a track meet

or band performance. We feel it is essential to make sacrifices to do things as a family.

For some years now I have taken our children out individually for lunch or dinner. I would recommend this practice for all families, and if you're financially strapped, take them for a coke or a milkshake. I ask questions about school or other interests that particular child may have, and I welcome their questions about what I am up to.

And be careful to maintain ties with your larger family. It is a tragedy when couples are needlessly alienated from their parents. If there are problems, work unceasingly at patching up that relationship. Your children need it, and you yourself need it.

For all of us, rootedness and security is closely related to our sense of family ties. When our children were young, we packed up the car every Christmas to make the long drive from Fort Worth, Texas, to Birmingham, Alabama—and later from points in Ohio and Tennessee to Birmingham—to be home for Christmas.

SECRET #4: BE BOTH FRIENDS AND LOVERS

GORDON: I can truly say that Mary Sue is my best friend. And I believe this is so because we have worked hard at communication and loving intimacy through the years. We know each other well enough to anticipate one another's feelings and responses.

There is a marriage triangle that helps build both love and friendship. This is the one in which Christ is the Head, the apex of the triangle. Then as we move up the sides of the triangle growing closer to Him, we grow closer to one another.

MARY SUE: The night we were married we started the custom of reading a passage of Scripture and praying together. I remember with strong emotions kneeling beside the bed and hearing my new husband thanking the Lord for me and our love and then asking God to cause our love for one another to grow. God has really answered that prayer.

Communication is the key to intimacy. Father Gordon and I *talk*. We share feelings, opinions, needs, and questions. Sometimes we shout, sometimes we cry, but most often we are on the same side of the issue. He is a night person, and often does his best work between 8:00 and 11:00 p.m. I cannot stay up after 10:00 and function, so I'm always in bed before he is. However, I usually wake up when he comes to bed, and many nights we spend an hour or so talking about the children, the ministry, and sometimes problems. (However, I don't recommend discussing problems at night—it robs you of your sleep!)

GORDON: Work at becoming a good lover.

I am aware that our narcissistic, hedonistic culture has placed too much emphasis on self-fulfillment and self-gratification. And in that vein, many marriage manuals seem to focus largely on sensual fulfillment. The danger is that one may come to see oneself as a failure if he hasn't achieved the status of a "super sex partner." Though some enter marriage with a need to learn and grow as lovers, this does not mean they are destined to permanent marital unhappiness or failure.

You *can* learn to become a lover—a good one. Remember, the essence of the Christian faith is redemption. We *are* capable of being changed—thank God! You can become a loving, thoughtful, caring partner. Take delight in the "wife [or husband] of your youth" (Proverbs 5:18). *Choose* to be warm and unselfish, giving and forgiving. These are the things that make physical love grow into something strong and healthy.

And may I hasten to say that Father Weldon Hardenbrook's book, *Missing From Action* [published through Conciliar Press], is as strong a statement as you'll find regarding the role of the husband in a healthy marriage.

DETERMINE TO BE DETERMINED ABOUT THE PERMANENCE OF YOUR MARRIAGE. NEVER GIVE UP LOVING EACH OTHER.

SECRET # 5: NEVER GIVE UP

MARY SUE: As a newly engaged couple, we made a determined effort to do all we could to make our marriage work out. Father Gordon asked his favorite religion professor at school to give us some premarital counseling. He talked to us only about an hour, but it was very helpful. He told us to bring our ideals down to meet the reality of our mate. He helped us have a more realistic view of marriage. We had no doubt we would be happy.

GORDON: The professor pointed out that if the two of us were stranded alone on a South Sea island, no matter how far apart we might initially be in our differences and ideals, ultimately we would come together for support and survival. We would find a way to live and work in harmony out of sheer necessity. I've never forgotten this.

We must live and act toward one another as if there are *no other alternatives*. Very few couples would develop marital differences and/or ultimately divorce one another if they didn't think there was someone better out there, or some better circumstance. If they viewed this partner as the *only one* for them, and this present union as their only hope for happiness, support, and survival, they would find ways to get along.

Perhaps one of the most important things to remember is *never talk about quitting*. There's something far superior, by the way, to the desert island for support in marriage. And that is our life within the One Holy Church. For our security is ultimately spiritual in nature. When you are rooted in a vital Church life, you will experience the protection, accountability, and sacramental security your marriage needs. The Orthodox Church is blessed with an incredibly strong sense of family rootedness and sanctity of marriage.

Determine to be determined about the permanence of your marriage. Never give up loving each other. Refuse to cave in to counter-suggestions from the devil. Practice saying and doing loving things. Even the beautiful and erotic plant of married love requires constant cultivation.

Also, never give up praying. When problems come, turn immediately to God in prayer. For the Christian, change is always possible, and "prayer changes things." Passivity in prayer can be lethal to a marriage.

Finally, never give up believing. Believe in God and His ability to make yours a good marriage. Believe in each other, let the Holy Spirit lead you together. Believe that change for the better is possible through Christ.

MARY SUE: And now, on to the joy of the next thirty-five years!

Fr. Gordon T. Walker is pastor of Saint Ignatius Orthodox Church in Franklin, Tennessee. He and Mary Sue have five adult children and many grandchildren.

From AGAIN Vol. 10, No. 2
Original publication date: June, 1987

Questions for thought and discussion:

1) Which of the three ways to "verbalize your love" do you *most* need to work on putting into practice: saying "forgive me"; saying "thank you"; or saying "I love you"? Think of several examples of times you have failed to say these things, and specific ways to improve in the future.

2) In your own family experience, were mealtimes treated as a sacrament and given high priority? Think of specific ways you will incorporate this concept into your marriage.

3) When is the best time of day (or time during the week) for you to have a regular time of communication and sharing?

4) Do you know of any couples whose marriages have failed, at least in part, because "quitting" was a talked-about option? Are you prepared to make a commitment that you will work to do everything possible to make this marriage endure?

THE FAMILY ALTAR
Establishing a Place of Prayer
by Deacon Michael Hyatt

As a young junior high school student, I wasn't fast enough to run most track and field events. But one event I could participate in was the relay race.

A large part of our training was concerned with *handing off the baton.* The idea was to sprint as fast as you could to the next runner on your team. His job was to meet you about fifteen yards before the handoff and run with you, being careful to match your pace exactly. In this way, you didn't have to stop to hand him the baton; you could continue the race without losing momentum. If everything went smoothly, the baton was passed from one hand to the next and the race progressed.

The handoff was the single most important part of the race. Not that it was that difficult, mind you; it just led to the worst of consequences if it wasn't managed properly. The running part was easy. You simply did your best and that was that. But the handoff had to be conducted with care lest—horror of horrors—you dropped the baton and thereby cost your team precious time and probably the race as well.

Running too slowly was excusable; all you could do was your best. But dropping the baton was totally unforgivable. Such a tragedy would lead to the immediate scorn of your teammates and the derision of your opponents. It was something that most all of us dreaded and worked to avoid.

Recently, I asked a group of young parents in our parish what their chief priority was with their children. Not surprisingly, each of them spoke of passing on their faith to their children. Like a runner in a relay race, no one wanted to stumble. The consequences of doing so were more than any of us wanted to consider.

But as a practical matter, how do we pass on our faith to our children? How do we successfully hand off our faith to the next generation so that they can continue the race and do their part to advance the Christian mission? No doubt, there are a variety of ways. But I would suggest that one of the main ones is the practice of family prayer.

THE HOME: Icon of the Church

As an Orthodox Christian I've come to believe that the Kingdom of God is the central reality of life. It takes precedence over every other allegiance, over every other priority. But that Kingdom is not some ethereal, faraway place. No, it is concretely manifested in the life of the Church, especially in the Divine Liturgy. In other words, if you want to experience the reality of the Kingdom, look at the Church, which is the principal icon of that Kingdom. But if this is true, of what significance is the Christian home? Does it have a role in Christ's Kingdom?

As a Protestant, I believed (though I would never have said it in quite this way) that the Church was an icon of the home. I was convinced that the Christian home was the central institution of society and everything else—even the Church—was secondary. But now, as an Orthodox Christian, I've come to believe that I had it all backwards: *the home is an icon of the Church.*

This is far more than some esoteric, theological point. It has important ramifications for our family life and especially for how we raise our children. Amazingly, this idea actually makes the home more important, not less. Let me elaborate.

In the Church, Christ has established a government made up of bishops, priests, and deacons. And in like manner, He has also established a government in the home: the parents, who are, in a very real sense, domestic priests. Consider the fact that the hymns sung at an Orthodox wedding as the bride and groom are led around the table are the very same ones sung at an ordination of a priest when he is led around the altar.

Parents, like priests in the Church, have a responsibility to shepherd the flock allotted to their charge (see 1 Peter 5:14). And as parents, we must rediscover our roles as domestic priests and our corresponding responsibility to pass on our faith to our children.

There are, of course, many more parallels between the Church and the home, but space permits me to mention just one: the centrality of the altar. The primary responsibility of a priest is to officiate at the altar. It is there that, representing the people, he brings their gifts of bread and wine before God's throne as an offering of praise and thanksgiving. And it is also there that, representing the Lord Himself, the priest returns to the people the holy food of Christ's flesh and blood. Similarly, the family altar should be the central feature of every Christian home and prayer its most important activity. The family altar is the primary place where we pass on to our children the "baton" of our faith.

But if this is true, what are some practical ways in which we can focus our family's activities on prayer?

THE FAMILY ALTAR:
A Place of Prayer

If you are to take your role as priest seriously, you must first of all construct an altar for your family. In order to do something well, you need a place to do it. Dad needs a place where he can fix broken bikes and build bird feeders. Mom needs a place where she can sew and mend clothing. The children need a place where they can play and make crafts. The family also needs a place to pray—the family altar.

This special place of prayer does not have to be fancy, but it does have to be special. Remember, it is a place where the family carries out its most vital activities: prayer, the reading of the sacred Scriptures, and the announcing of important events in the life of the family.

While each family's altar will be uniquely theirs, most altars share certain common characteristics. Usually the altar faces the East. From ancient times Christians have seen in the rising of the sun a symbolic representation of the coming of Christ, the Sun of Justice (see Malachi 4:2). The altar can be a simple shelf mounted on a wall, a small table covered with a tablecloth or, as in my family's case, a special dresser with a glass top. Regardless of the form it takes, most family altars include certain basic components: a few icons on the wall or on the altar itself, candles, a Bible, and prayer books. Optional items include a small incense burner, candle snuffer, and a bottle of Holy Water.

When is the right time to gather at the family altar? Any time, of course. But through the centuries, Christians have especially gathered twice a day for corporate prayer: morning and evening. Morning prayer gives us an opportunity to bring our needs and concerns to God before we embark on the day's activities. It also helps each person "set his mind on the things above" (Colossians 3:1) where he can address the bustle and demands of the day from a spiritual frame of reference. Evening prayer, on the other hand, is an opportunity for us to review the day, confess where we have failed, and to give thanks where we have succeeded.

Prayer during these two times does not have to be long; ten to fifteen minutes is generally sufficient. The important thing is to be consistent. It's far better to spend five minutes a day *every* day praying together than to spend fifteen or twenty minutes praying a couple of times a week. The general principle is to become faithful in little before we stretch ourselves—and our family!—to become faithful in much (see Luke 16:10).

There are, of course, other times to pray. Whenever there is a special need in the family it's a good practice to stop what we're doing and gather for a few

---

A Morning Prayer:

Arising from sleep, I thank You, O Holy Trinity, that, for the sake of Your great kindness and long-suffering, You have not had indignation against me, for I am slothful and sinful. Neither have You destroyed me in my transgressions, but You have shown Your customary love towards man and have raised me up as I lay in heedlessness, that I might sing my morning hymn and glorify Your Sovereignty. Enlighten the eyes of my heart, open my mouth to meditate on Your words, and teach me Your commandments. Help me to do Your will, to hymn You, to confess You from my heart, and to extol Your all-holy Name, of the Father, Son, and Holy Spirit, now and ever, and unto ages of ages. Amen.

An Evening Prayer:

O eternal God, King of all creation, who has vouchsafed me to attain to this hour, forgive me the sins which I have committed this day in thought, word, and deed, and cleanse, O Lord, my humble soul from every stain of flesh and spirit. Grant me, O Lord, to pass through the sleep of this night in peace, to rise from my lowly bed, and to please Your holy Name all the days of my life, and to vanquish the enemies both corporeal and incorporeal that contend against me. Deliver me, O Lord, from the vain thoughts that stain me, and from evil desires. For Yours is the Kingdom, and the power, and the glory, of the Father, and of the Son, and of the Holy Spirit, now and ever, and unto ages of ages. Amen.

moments at the family altar. In like manner, whenever something especially good happens, it's a good idea to stop and give thanks. These times of spontaneous prayer are wonderful tools for communicating to children the reality of God's presence and His involvement in our lives.

Once you've selected the appropriate time and place, you still have one important decision left to make: what to pray at the family altar. For many people this is the most difficult. Fortunately, there are a variety of resources available to help us. Good prayer books can be obtained from a variety of Orthodox publishing houses. Regardless of which one you use, try to get a copy for each member of your family. This will encourage everyone's participation and give you, as the leader, the option of calling on various members of the family to lead in certain prayers (something my children love to do).

When using a prayer book, it is not necessary to say every prayer, nor is it necessary to "stick to the script." If you're just starting out or if your children are small (and their attention spans short), you might want to pray only the Trisagion Prayers, have a short time for extemporaneous personal petitions, and then go immediately to the dismissal. In my house we often use the prayers as a springboard for our own prayers. This is especially true when we're praying what are referred to as the General Intercessions. For example, if we're praying for the whole Church, we might pause after the written prayer and pray spontaneously for the specific needs of our local parish. Similarly, if we're praying for the civil authorities, we might pause and pray for specific needs in our own community. In this way, prayer becomes a living, dynamic activity rather than a dull, repetitive one. To me, this is liturgical prayer at its best.

One final note: prayer was never intended to be a monologue. In genuine prayer God speaks to us, and we speak to Him. Both are necessary for dialogue. But how does God speak to us? Are we to expect an audible voice? Generally, God speaks to us through the reading of the Holy Scriptures. Thus, Bible reading should be an integral part of our family worship. God specifically charges parents to have His Word upon their hearts and then to pass it on to their children (see Deuteronomy 6:4-9). What better context for Bible reading than as we are gathered together as a family for the purpose of prayer?

> **"The family altar is the primary place where we pass on to our children the 'baton' of our faith."**

A FEW MISCELLANEOUS TIPS

In conclusion, let me give you three brief tips, items that will go a long way toward making your family's experience at the family altar a meaningful one.

1. Start small. You can't run a marathon without training and neither can you engage in long prayers without training yourself in the short ones.

2. Be sensitive to your children's attention spans. Yes, it's good to stretch them, but don't break them! The last thing you want is for prayer to be something your children dread. Again, it's far better to keep it brief and meaningful than to frustrate your children—and ultimately yourself—by reading long drawn-out prayers. Remember, the Publican was justified with a very short prayer: "God be merciful to me a sinner." And the thief on the cross entered Paradise with one sentence: "Remember me, O Lord, when You come into Your Kingdom."

3. Let everyone participate. Although you will be tempted, don't insist on doing everything yourself. Make sure everyone has a book (even the little ones that can't read), and let your children lead some of the prayers. If they can read, let them read the Scripture lessons. If you follow this principle, you'll find that they look forward to prayer and, little by little, begin to own it as *their* prayer.

Deacon Michael Hyatt
Nashville, Tennessee

From AGAIN Vol. 12, No. 1.
Original publication date: March, 1989

FOR FURTHER READING:

Let me recommend two books:
- A *Guide for the Domestic Church* (published by the Diocese of Newton [Melkite Catholic], Office of Educational Services, 19 Dartmouth Street, West Newton, MA 01265); and
- *Making God Real in the Orthodox Home* by Father Anthony Coniaris (published by Light and Life Publishing Company, 4836 Park Glen Road, Minneapolis, MN 55416).

Both of these books offer a vast array of practical advice for Orthodox parents who want to make their home truly a *Christian* home.

Questions for thought and discussion:

1) What are your current practices of personal prayer? Do you keep a regular prayer rule? When? Where? How long do you usually pray?

2) How do you plan to coordinate your times of personal prayer, if you will be using the same prayer altar?

3) Have you already made plans to establish a family altar in your new home? What will it include? Where will it be located?

4) How often and at what times do you plan to come together for family prayer? Which prayers will you say together? Which prayers will be said by the husband? by the wife? Will you incorporate Bible reading into your family prayer time?

5) What do you plan for meal-time prayers? Which prayers will be said, and who will lead them?

6) How do you foresee your family prayer time changing when you have children? How do you plan to teach your children to pray?

7) How do you plan to celebrate namedays, feast days, and other special events as a family? How will you tie these events to worship around your family altar?

DOES
EQUAL
MEAN
THE
SAME?

by Fr. John Weldon
Hardenbrook

Is the president of the United States of greater worth than the Secret Service agent who guards him? Does Lee Iacocca have more innate dignity than the janitor who cleans his office at Chrysler Corporation headquarters? Does *MS.* magazine's Gloria Steinem have more human worth than the magazine's newest staff proofreader?

To all of the above, of course, the answer is a resounding no!

A human being's value is not found in office or function. Human worth is described by the phrase *imago Dei,* which means each of us is made in the image of God. Each person—male or female, rich or poor, famous or obscure—has the same value as the next. No one has any more or less. The differences that exist between the president and the Secret Service agent, between Lee Iacocca

and the janitor, and between Gloria Steinem and the proofreader have nothing to do with human worth. The differences are not in value, but in function.

It is obvious that Chrysler Corporation's Board of Directors would have a more difficult time replacing Mr. Iacocca than the janitor who cleans his office. And it is understatement to say that Iacocca is more important to the success of Chrysler than the entirety of their custodial staff. But in terms of innate human worth, things are quite different. In the eyes of the God who created and offers redemption to both Mr. Iacocca and the custodian, each of them has identical value.

It is all too easy for the janitor to feel that because he has a less prestigious and lower-paying job, he is not as valuable a person as the man whose office he cleans each night. But to hold such a view is to give in to the mistaken idea which falsely equates human value with function.

BONE OF CONTENTION

A tremendous amount of tension in the realm of male and female relationships has arisen in recent years because of this tragic tendency to equate value and function. Often the precise point of contention is the historical understanding that ultimate responsibility for leadership in human relationships lies with men. Once universally accepted in the Church, this belief has come under attack in recent years by those who claim that to grant such leadership to men is to say that women are of inferior value.

Such a view has in fact gained wide acceptance. But such a view is also a novelty in the long history of God's people. Through most of her history, there was broad agreement in the Church that Scripture teaches that the ultimate responsibility for leadership belongs to men (1 Corinthians 11:3; Ephesians 5:23).

But with a contempt for the wisdom of the past that only we arrogant moderns seem able to mount, recent years have witnessed a host of attempts to dismiss the consensus of God's people throughout the years as archaic and culturally inapplicable. Never mind that to reinterpret the passages of Scripture in question requires one to be a hermeneutical contortionist. Men and women are increasingly bowing to the pressures of modern culture and rejecting male leadership.

Masculine leadership is, of course, the biblical truth that feminists—male and female, Christian and non-Christian alike—hate the most. And a groundswell of reaction against this foundational reality in the Scriptures is already producing a whole new genera-

tion, both in the world and in much of Christendom. For this reason a feminist declaration, "The Document," charges, "Marriage has existed for the benefit of men and has been a legally sanctioned method of control over women . . . the end of the institution of marriage is a necessary condition for the liberation of women."

A MODERN MISCONCEPTION

Why are some people so offended at the idea of male leadership that they would call for the abolition of marriage? I am convinced that it is due to a gross misunderstanding of the concept of headship and a confusion between value and function.

Headship relates to function, and has nothing whatsoever to do with value. If having the leadership role made the male of the species innately more valuable, something would indeed be terribly unjust. But giving men the position of family head does not mean that women are of less value than men. The biblically prescribed headship of the husband in human families has nothing to do with men being of greater worth than women, for they are not. The issue is the office or function that God has assigned to each.

Men who actually think they are more valuable because God asks them to be the head of the family unit are deceived. And women who feel reduced in personhood because they are not in charge are equally mistaken.

THE ULTIMATE EXAMPLE

Suppose I were to tell you that my life was totally under the direction of someone else. Suppose I were to expand upon that statement by telling you that person had so much authority in my life that he told me what to do and even what to say; that I did nothing on my own initiative. Would you be willing to believe that, even though all the foregoing was true, I was absolutely equal to this person?

I have just described the relationship that Jesus said exists between Himself and God the Father (see John 5:19; 5:30; 6:38; 7:16; 8:28; 12:49; 14:10). The relationship that exists between two of the three divine Persons of the Holy Trinity is the perfect model by which we can gain a right understanding of the relationship between function and value in human affairs (see Philippians 2:5-8).

In the Trinity we find that God the Father is the head, but this headship does not make the Son of less value. The Father and the Son are equal. You see, if function (in Christ's case, becoming a man) made Him less in value than the Father, He could not be God! But on the contrary, He is, based on both Holy Scripture and the Nicene Creed, God of God, Light of Light, the only begotten Son, our Lord Jesus Christ, eternally generated from the Father. *He has no less value because he has a different function.*

Herein lies the answer for people who are confused by equating function and value. If we will accept the Trinitarian relationship within the Godhead as a pattern for us humans, it will put an end to the frantic "climbing of ladders" to prove one's worth. We as human beings are loved and valued by God because we are made by Him. Having been created in His image, we have the real basis for our worth as persons. Headship, then, does not make one more valuable. Rather, it has been ordained from God the Father, the very source of the blessed Trinity, to assure us of peace, order, and equality.

PASSIVITY AND DOUBLE STANDARDS

Without headship, anarchy reigns. Primacy is absolutely necessary for peace in human relationships. Even feminists know this. That's why *MS.* magazine has an executive editor and also why the National Organization for Women has a president.

Headship is also essential to the health of the family. Unfortunately, since the Victorian era, headship in the American family has been hotly contested. And most of the fault for such a situation lies, not with women, but with men. The tension between American men and women exists primarily because men have increasingly left their heavenly model of headship and have ceased to exercise proper leadership in their homes.

HAVING BEEN CREATED IN HIS IMAGE, WE HAVE THE REAL BASIS FOR OUR WORTH AS PERSONS.

At best, headship in families is often up for grabs. The homes of our land have become battlefields for domestic power struggles. Nevertheless, the *ultimate* responsibility for decision making within marriage is to be with the husband. This does not mean women are not to make decisions. All it means is that the *ultimate* responsibility for moral leadership in the home, and all commensurate decisions, should normally be the responsibility of the father.

Why does this sound so unfair to contemporary ears? I believe it is because of husbands who demand the submission of their wives, but in turn submit to no one but themselves! Just as a real man is to be the head of his family, he is also supposed to be under authority himself.

I don't blame the frustrated women who feel the injustice of being under the headship of men who aren't accountable anywhere. It's not fair, and it's also not Christian. Yes, the husband is the head of the wife, but the husband is to be accountable to the leaders of the Church. To family leaders the Scripture says, "Obey those who rule over you, and be submissive, for they watch out for your souls, as those who must give account" (Hebrews 13:17).

Now that's fair! In this kind of relationship a woman has a court of appeal if she is treated wrongly, which is, by the way, exactly how American women were once ensured of justice. In the earliest days of American settlement, women could find justice even in very personal matters. For example, history tells us of the husband of a colonial woman who refused to engage in intercourse with his wife for a period of two years. The wife complained to the Church. The Church leaders pleaded with the man to repent and care for his wife. He refused and was excommunicated from the Church. Stubborn guys finish last! There was a time when men were accountable for how they treated women.

Unfortunately such is no longer the case. In refusing to submit to the headship of their husbands, American wives are merely copying the example of their men, who refused to submit to the headship of Christ as expressed through His Church.

Like begets like. Feminism is but a response to men's refusal to exercise the headship God calls them to, or to their exercising leadership over others without being accountable themselves.

The issue of headship will cease to be a point of great debate in this land when American culture stops erroneously equating a person's function with his or her human worth. And it will cease to be a point of friction between the sexes when men who ask women to follow them are equally intent on following the headship of Christ, as expressed in the leadership He has ordained in His Church.

Portions of this article are adapted from a chapter in Fr. Hardenbrook's book Missing From Action (*originally published by Thomas Nelson in 1987; revised edition published by Conciliar Press in 1996*).

Fr. John Weldon Hardenbrook
Editor, AGAIN Magazine

From AGAIN Vol. 10, No. 2.
Original publication date: June, 1987

Questions for thought and discussion:

1) On what sources do you base your own feelings of personal worth or value? Do you have a real sense of your worth being based upon the truth that you were made in the image of God? If not, how can you achieve this?

2) How does each of you view the male-headship role in the home? Give several practical applications of how you would like to see the "office" of headship function in your marriage relationship.

3) How does each of you view the role of the headship of Christ, as expressed through leadership in the Church? How can you avoid possible frustrations caused by a "double standard"?

IMAGO DEI

THE BASIS OF OUR WORTH

By Fr. Thomas Hopko

There is much discussion these days concerning the essence of Christianity, much talk about what the Gospel of Jesus Christ is really about. For Orthodox Christians the answer is clear. The heart of our Christian faith is that the invisible God has become visible in the Person of Jesus Christ.

The Holy Scriptures call Jesus Christ the image—or icon—of the invisible God (Colossians 1:15). God who cannot be seen is now seen in the Person of Jesus. The Lord Himself declares this when He says to Philip: "He who has seen Me has seen the Father" (John 14:9). In Jesus Christ, the Incarnate Son and Word, God has shown Himself to the world in the most perfect way that He can.

What makes Christianity different from every other religion, philosophy, teaching, and way of life is that in the Person of Christ, God's Son—who is also God's Word, Wisdom, Radiance, Glory, Truth, Light, Life, and Power—has become flesh.

God has become man. The Eternal Son has assumed human nature. He has done this so that we could be what we were made to be in the beginning: creatures made in God's image and likeness for unending life in communion with Him.

God's plan for us, as the saints have said, is that we become by His divine grace everything that He Himself is by nature. Human beings who are created, redeemed, and sanctified by God through Christ and the Holy Spirit are made "gods by grace," holy as God Himself is holy, citizens of paradise, co-rulers with Christ in God's Kingdom. We not only come thereby to know God, we come to know ourselves in our true being and destiny as children of the Most High, creatures made in His image and likeness to live His divine life now, in the world, and forever.

LOVED AND LOVERS

If we humans are made in God's image, according to His likeness, we are created to be loved by God, and so ourselves to become lovers, loving with the very love with which God—who is Love—loved us. This is our calling as human beings. When Christ comes to the world and pours His divine love, the love of His Father, into our hearts by the Holy Spirit (Romans 5:5), we are empowered to love with His very own love.

Jesus Christ not only gives the commandment to love, He manifests what love really is. He actualizes it perfectly in His own human life. And He gives the power of this love to His disciples in the gift of the Spirit.

Christ's "new commandment," therefore, is not simply to love. To love is the "old commandment" which we have "from the beginning" (1 John 2:7). To love is the central commandment in the Law of Moses (Deuteronomy 6:5; Leviticus 19:18). To love is the teaching of every religion and philosophy born of purity and light.

Christ's "new commandment" is not simply that we are to love, but that we are to love one another, as He declared, "as I have loved you" (John 13:34). This is the radical new part: that we are to love everyone, including our worst enemies, as Christ Himself has loved us. And how does He love us? Completely, wholly, perfectly, absolutely, boundlessly, without reservation or condition.

THE IMAGE IS PLURAL

According to the Scriptures, human beings can find and fulfill themselves as made in God's image and likeness only in loving union with others. We are persons in communion with other persons, just like the Persons of the Holy Trinity: Father, Son, and Holy Spirit.

The uniqueness of God, according to the Christian revelation, is that He is Father by nature. He is not alone in His divinity. Indeed, He cannot be. God is Love, and therefore He has a divine Son according to His very being as God. He also has a personal Holy Spirit who proceeds from Him as God and rests eternally in His uncreated Son. The Godhead is a community of Persons from all eternity. Divinity is three Persons in an identity of being and life.

This is what the Nicene Creed means when it says that the Son of God is "begotten of the Father before all ages . . . begotten not created . . . of one essence with the Father," the divine Son and Word "by whom all things are made." And that the Holy Spirit is "the Lord and Life-giver" who is "worshiped and glorified with the Father and the Son."

We human beings express, in creaturely form, the very being of God. We too are persons of the same nature, "of one essence" with each other. We too are to form a perfect community of love. The Church of Christ is just such a community, a communion of truth and love, a plurality of persons in perfect unity: one mind, one heart, one soul, one body with each other and with God through the humanity of our Lord—and our friend and brother—Jesus Christ.

In this light it is critical to see and to understand that there is no such thing as an "individual." The modern "individual," I've come to believe, is an invention of some European intellectual: a total fiction. There simply is no such thing as an "individual." There are only persons in communion with other persons in the likeness of God Himself; for the Blessed Trinity is hardly a trio of "individuals" in "mutually fulfilling relationships." The Godhead is rather Three divine Persons in a perfect unity of being and life, the content of which is Love.

Human beings can be "individuals" if they choose, with all kinds of "relationships." But if they do so choose, to use the language of the Bible, they choose death, and not life; the curse and not the blessing (Deuteronomy 30:19). They destroy themselves in the act of metaphysical suicide in their self-contained and self-interested isolation which is the very image of hell. The word "individual," it might be pointed out, comes from the Greek word "itself" or "one's own," from which we also get the English word "idiot." There is a message here which should not go unheeded.

When we live in God's way, we live in communion with others. When we are saved, we are saved with others. We are members of one another (Ephesians 4:16). We are not our own; we belong to one another (1 Corinthians 6:19; 12:12-27). We love our neighbor as our self because he or she is our very self. We find our self in the other through an act of self-emptying, self-denying love. This is our very nature, made this way by God who finds and fulfills His own divine Self in this very same way. We can doubt and deny this basic truth if we wish, but we do so to our destruction and death.

THE IMAGE IS MALE AND FEMALE

Not only are we human beings persons in communion with other persons, but we are also persons created to be male and female, men and women. Gender difference is part of our human nature as made in God's image and likeness. This does not mean that there is gender in God. God is not male or female. He is not a man or a woman. Indeed, God is not even a "being" if we think of Him as being the way we are in any sense at all. As Saint Gregory Palamas put it, "If God is being, I am not; if I am being, God is not." By this he obviously meant that we cannot speak of the uncreated God and the created world in the same way, using the words in the same sense. But the Scripture does say that God made us male and female in His own image and likeness, thus indicating that our sexuality is at the very heart of our being made for loving communion in imitation of God (Genesis 1:26, 27).

The first "no good" from the mouth of God in the Bible is when He looks at Adam alone. God separates the light from the darkness and calls it good. He brings forth the various plants and animals and calls them good. He puts the sun and moon and stars in the heavens and calls them good. Indeed all is good; very good. But man alone is no good: "It is not good that man should be alone" (Genesis 2:18). So Adam is placed in a deep sleep and from his side comes woman: flesh of his flesh and bone of his bones, the completion of his humanity. And this, the saints teach, is an image of Christ and the Church, the new Adam and the new Eve who become "one flesh" in the mystery of salvation.

There is nothing essential to human nature that does not belong equally to men and women. And there is nothing in the redeemed humanity of Christ and the Church that is not equally the possession of women and men. This is the meaning of the famous passage of Saint Paul that in Christ "there is neither Jew nor Greek, there is neither slave nor free, there is neither male nor female" but that we are "all one in Christ" (Galatians 3:28).

According to the Old Covenant Law, there were radical differences between men and women in their relationship to the Lord; just as there were fundamental differences between Jews and Greeks, slaves and freemen. But as we sing at our Orthodox baptismal service, as well as at the eucharistic liturgies on the most festive occasions, from the same apostolic epistle: "As many . . . as were baptized into Christ have put on Christ" (Galatians 3:27). In the New Covenant

"Of what use is existence to the creature if it cannot know its Maker? How could men be reasonable beings if they had no knowledge of the Word and reason of the Father?. . . Why should God have made [men] at all, if He had not intended them to know Him? But, in fact, the good God has given them a share in His own Image, that is, in our Lord Jesus Christ, and has made even them after the same Image and Likeness.

"Why? Simply in order that through this gift of God-likeness in themselves they may be able to perceive the Image Absolute, that is the Word Himself, and through Him to apprehend the Father; which knowledge of their Maker is for men the only really happy and blessed life."
—Saint Athanasius

"You are not much different from cattle, except that you have intelligence; so do not glory in anything else. Do you claim to be strong? You will be beaten by beasts. Do you claim speed? Flies are faster. Do you claim beauty? What great beauty there is in a peafowl's feathers! How are you better, then, than these? By the image of God."
—Saint Augustine

"In six days God made the world: but the world was for man. The sun was resplendent with bright beams, yet was made to give light to man, yea and all living creatures were formed to serve us: herbs and trees were created for our enjoyment. All the works of creation were good, but none of these was an image of God, save man only."
—Saint Cyril of Jerusalem

in Christ, the age of the "new creation" in the Messiah, there is the same calling, the same mission and the same judgment for all—even though there is not the same function and ministry in those aspects of life which are specifically masculine and feminine, such as fatherhood and motherhood in families and church communities.

The question often arises on this issue about unmarried men and women. Do they image God in their celibate condition? The answer of the Church is certain and clear: They do; but only on condition that they are not unmarried because they despise sexuality and are unable to relate positively to others on the sexual level. There are canons in the Church from the fourth century (Council of Gangra) which rule that if any person enters the monastic life because of contempt for sexuality and marriage, or for the body and matter generally, they are not only to be put out of the monastic life, they are to be put out of the communion of the Church as heretics. In fact all of the unmarried saints of the Church, including those in the monastic life, lived in healthy spiritual communion with persons of the opposite sex—and their own sex as well. They would not have been holy had this not been the case.

WHERE A MAN BELONGS

Our godly behavior, our self-understanding as human beings, is only fully possible in communion with Christ in the community of the Church which is His Body. In Christ and the Church we know who we are as men and women. We know why we were made, and why we were made the way we are. We know our task and our calling. We know our destiny as creatures. We know these things because in Christ and the Church, by the power of His Spirit, we know God: the source, ground, and goal of our being and life—the very life of our life—the One in whose image and likeness we are made.

Human hearts are made "toward God," Saint Augustine said, and "are restless until they rest in Him." Only when we find God and abide in Him are we satisfied and fulfilled as human beings. This is surely the basic reason for the discontent, dissatisfaction, confusion, and frustration in the modern world, particularly in America. This is devastatingly revealed, in my opinion, in contemporary advertising.

When cigarette ads, for example, present their products as "spirit" (Salem) and "alive with pleasure" (Newport) and "the experience you seek" (Kent), it can only indicate one thing. What the ad people have discovered, undoubtedly through extensive analysis and research, is that these "pseudo-mysteries" are the greatest needs of their prospective customers. The prize-winner is surely the Camel ad where the gorgeous machoman in flannel shirt and jeans is sitting on a rock in a sylvan setting exactly in the posture of the famous sculpture of Rodin, "The Thinker," meditating in solitude beneath an "icon" of a pack of Camels. The "good news" is proclaimed in the printed message: "Camels—Where a man belongs!"

The Camel Filter ad says simply: "Camel Filters: A Whole New World!"

What does all this mean? What is it saying? To me it says loudly and clearly: Contemporary man is devoid of spirit, is unhappy and dead, is seeking a satisfying experience, because he doesn't know who he is or where he belongs. What he really wants is a whole new world. To solve his problem he need only smoke the right cigarette—ignoring in the process, of course, the Surgeon General's grim warning.

A CONSUMING FIRE

It is easy to look at others, to ridicule the world, to satirize the materialists, to poke fun at the faithless. But what about us Christians? What are we looking for? What do we want? Where is our treasure? Where do we belong? In what world do we live? We say that we believe in God, and that we believe that we are made in God's image and likeness for an unending divine life that begins already here on earth. But do we really?

A priest once came to me for confession and counsel with the following story. There was a couple in his parish, each of whom was well over eighty years old. They had been extremely active in the church their whole lives. They had, I remember him saying, about a hundred and fifty combined years of church singing and service. When the community arranged a tribute to the couple, with a gift of thanksgiving for their faithful participation over the many decades, the couple was invited to say a few words. The woman began by accusing the people of overlooking their sacrifices, chided them for their failures, pointed out in detail "all we have done," and bitterly reprimanded them for their lack of attention and gratitude. The priest was stunned by this, as were the people of the church. Such was the result of a century and a half of active church membership!

How can this be explained? The answer again is clear. The couple was not there for God. They were there for other reasons: to play a role, to be the "ones who come," to check who didn't come, to satisfy their own sense of service, to wield power, to insure that things are being done the way they want, to satisfy their craving for involvement. The list of reasons is potentially endless. But love for God and neighbor in secret, sacrificial, self-emptying service is not one of them.

And this, as Bishop Theophan the Recluse in last-century Russia once said, is why so many of us who are actively involved in Church become worse instead of better for our involvement: more judgmental instead of merciful, angry instead of peaceful, irritated instead of serene, upset instead of joyful, suspicious instead of generous, bitter instead of happy, despondent instead of beautiful and full of light. We simply are not in it for God. And this destroys us. For "our" God, as the bishop pointed out from the Scriptures, is a "consuming fire" (Hebrews 12:29). And one cannot play with divine fire, using and abusing it for one's own purposes, without being consumed.

We are made in God's image and likeness. We are made to be loved and to love. We are made to become Love by Love's presence in our lives. We are made to be by grace what our Lord is by nature. We are made to love with the very love with which God in Christ has loved us by the power of God's Holy Spirit.

If this is what we really believe, if this is what we really want, we will struggle for it daily, fighting the good fight to the end with gratitude and gladness. If not, our very involvement in the Church will consume us like stubble.

May the Lord, whose image we bear and whose likeness we are called to actualize ever more perfectly, inspire us to accept and to complete our high calling in Him. There is no greater joy in heaven and on earth. And no other life worthy of the name. We have been created for this alone. May we find and fulfill our true destiny—to God's glory and our own.

Fr. Thomas Hopko,
Dean, St. Vladimir's Seminary,
Crestwood, New York

From AGAIN Vol. 10, No. 2.
Original publication date: June, 1987

Questions for thought and discussion:

1) If our calling as human beings is to love others with the love with which Christ loved us, give examples of how you can apply this to married love? to love of children? to love of in-laws? Think of how you can make use of the situations provided in these relationships to grow in Christ-likeness.

2) Contrast Fr. Hopko's teaching that there is "no such thing as an 'individual.' There are only persons in communion with other persons in the likeness of God Himself" with modern society's stress on individual rights and self-fulfillment.

3) Try to put in your own words the Orthodox teaching regarding the differences/ similarities in the "calling" of men and women, and the differences/ similarities in the "roles" of men and women. How does this basic theology relate to your own understanding of femininity and masculinity?

ON TITHING

PUT GOD FIRST IN YOUR FINANCIAL PLANS

By Deacon Michael Hyatt

At our home, we are trying to teach our children the grace of giving. We always make sure they have something to put into the offering plate on Sunday morning. Even if it's only a quarter—which it generally is—we want them to learn that giving is part of the worship they offer to God.

On a recent Sunday, I gave my two-year-old daughter, Mary, a few coins and instructed her to place them in the collection plate at the appropriate time. As usual she was delighted and played happily with the coins in her hands.

When it was time to give, I saw Mary look at her coins and then look back at the collection plate. Suddenly, she had a flash of insight. As her older sister held the plate, Mary quietly set her coins aside and deftly thrust her hands past the checks and bills to the bottom of the plate. There her tiny fingers located the sought-for treasure—handfuls of shiny quarters, dimes, nickels, and pennies.

Without a twinge of guilt, she closed both fists around the coins, lifted them from the plate, and deposited them with her own. By this time, I noticed what was going on and stopped her cold as her hands went in for a second helping. Having no idea why she couldn't just help herself to what had obviously been offered to her, she began to protest loudly as the other children and adults near us laughed out loud.

HANDS IN THE OFFERING JAR

What is often cute in the behavior of a child is pathetic if it persists into adulthood. Yet thousands—perhaps millions—of Christians who would never consider taking money from the collection plate are systematically robbing God. How? Listen to the Lord as He addresses the nation of Israel: " 'Will a man rob God? Yet you have robbed Me! But you say, "In what way have we robbed You?" In tithes and offerings. You are cursed with a curse, for you have robbed Me, even this whole nation. Bring all the tithes into the storehouse, that there may be food in My house, and try Me now in this,' says the LORD of hosts, 'if I will not open for you the windows of heaven and pour out for you such blessing that there will not be room enough to receive it' " (Malachi 3:8-10).

In this passage, God accuses His people of robbing Him because they had failed to bring Him their tithes and offerings. This is a very serious charge. It's one thing to rob men, using either deceit or force to appropriate to ourselves that which belongs to another. But to rob God? This is an enormous crime!

THE BIBLICAL BASIS OF GIVING

In order to understand how God could possibly equate failure to pay tithes and offerings with robbery, we must grasp three biblical principles of stewardship.

1) Everything belongs to God. Because God created all things, He automatically owns all things: "The earth is the LORD's, and all its fullness, the world and those who dwell therein. For He has founded it upon the seas, and established it upon the waters" (Psalm 24:1, 2).

God owns it all. The cattle on a thousand hills (see Psalm 50:10) and even the hills themselves (see Psalm 50:12). But more importantly, He owns you and me: "For you were bought at a price; therefore glorify God in your body and in your spirit, which are God's" (1 Corinthians 6:20).

He is thus the true owner of everything we have. Not just our bodies and spirits, but our houses and cars, our pots and pans, our furniture and fixtures, our televisions and stereos, our children and pets, and even our bank accounts and IRAs. Nothing is exempt. God owns it all.

But if everything belongs to God, then where does that leave us? Isn't there anything that we can call our own?

2) We are God's stewards. God has placed each of us over *some* of His possessions. Our role is not that of an *owner* but that of a *steward*. Webster's *New World Dictionary* defines the term *steward* like this: "One who acts as a supervisor or administrator, as of finances and property, for another or others."

God has made some of us stewards over a large estate. He has made others of us stewards over a small estate. But make no mistake about it, all of us are stewards. This brings us to a third principle.

3) We are held accountable for how we use the resources God gives us. In the Parable of the Talents (see Matthew 25:14-30), our Lord makes it clear that He regards as "faithful" those who wisely use the resources He gives them. Conversely, he regards as "unfaithful" those who squander their opportunities and use His resources foolishly. The point of the parable is that for all of us there is an ultimate accountability in the exercise of our stewardship. We are not free to spend our money as we please. Nor are we free to invest our money as we please. Everything must be done to the glory of God and with a view to the reality that we will one day—at the dread judgment seat of Christ—give an account of our stewardship.

TITHES AND OFFERINGS IN THE OLD TESTAMENT

Early in their pilgrimage God revealed the importance of tithes and offerings to the Israelites. Certain offerings were required by the Law of Moses and were a non-optional facet of Old Testament belief and worship. Others were "free-will." These were given by the people as tokens of their gratitude and love towards God.

The tithe was also revealed in the Old Testament. Before God had given the Law through Moses, Abraham paid a tenth of all he had to Melchizedek, priest of God Most High (see Genesis 14:18-20). Then, through Moses, God revealed to His people that they were to set aside a tenth of what they produced each year (Deuteronomy 14:22-29; 26:12-15). This tithe—which literally means "a tenth"—was used for three specific purposes: 1) to support the Levitical priesthood (Numbers 18:21); 2) to celebrate the Lord's bounty in an annual feast (Deuteronomy 14:22-27); and 3) to care for the poor and fatherless (Deuteronomy 14:28, 29).

Even the Old Covenant *clergy* were required to pay a tenth of what they received to the central sanctuary in Jerusalem (Numbers 18:25-29)! Throughout the Old Testament, God admonished His people to pay the tithe and thus honor Him with their wealth (see e.g. Proverbs 3:9, 10). For them, the tithe was a kind of "tax" which they paid to God for the privilege of using the land He had given them. Consequently, when they failed to pay the tithe, God accused them of robbery and brought a curse upon the whole nation (Malachi 3:8-12).

TITHING IN THE NEW TESTAMENT

One of the most interesting New Testament passages in this regard is the story of Jesus' confrontation with the scribes and Pharisees over the issue of tithing. In Matthew 23:23, He says the following: "Woe to you, scribes and Pharisees, hypocrites! For you pay tithe of mint and anise and cummin, and have neglected the weightier matters of the law: justice and mercy and faith. *These you ought to have done, without leaving the others undone*" (emphasis mine).

The scribes and Pharisees took the Law of Moses very seriously. So seriously, in fact, that they paid a tithe on everything—even ordinary kitchen spices! However, in their zeal for the details, they lost sight of the big picture.

They failed to show justice and mercy and faith to their fellow man. Consequently, Jesus roundly condemned them.

But notice what He says. He tells them they should have done the greater things of the law (justice and mercy and faith) *without neglecting the lesser things* (tithing). He doesn't condemn their tithing—far from it! He actually applauds it. What he condemns is their failure to exercise the greater virtues.

Many things can be said about tithing in historic Orthodoxy. There were times when the tithe was used, and there were times when the practice disappeared altogether. For many years the state gave a percentage of taxes collected from the people directly to the Church, thereby alleviating the need for a direct tithe. At other times, no tax was given to the Church, yet the tithe was not revived.

One accusation, however, cannot be made against tithing. The Lord never condemned or forbade its use, nor did He call an end to the practice as an archaic facet of Old Covenant worship.

THE FOLLY OF NOT GIVING

When Gail and I were married we were taught the importance of giving to the Church. We were pretty much convinced that giving a ten-percent tithe of our income was a good idea. But as with so many good ideas, we weren't very faithful in its implementation. We gave, but only sporadically. After all the bills were paid, and if there was anything left over, we wrote a check to the Church. We kept the "first fruits." God got the leftovers. We knew it wasn't right, but we were convinced that we just couldn't afford to tithe. We hoped that someday we would make enough money so that there would be at least ten percent left over for God.

Everything went along fairly well until we discovered that Gail was pregnant with our first child. A few months before the baby came, she quit her job as a school teacher and became a full-time wife and mother. Unfortunately, like many couples, we had become dependent on two incomes. Fortunately, we still had all our credit cards. That's when the trouble began. Woe to the family that has more plastic than cash!

The first thing that got cut out of the budget was our check to the Church. A well-meaning Christian friend even encouraged us in this by saying, "You can't afford to give right now. Once you're a little more established in your career, you can start giving again." This was the worst advice we'd ever received.

Things went from bad to worse. The bills began to pile up. The car broke down. We had to buy clothes for the baby. I took a new job and had to buy some new suits. One thing led to another. Before long, we were under serious financial pressure. It eventually got to the point that we were afraid to go to the mailbox for fear there would be another past due notice or bill we couldn't pay.

Finally, one morning as I was reading the Scriptures, I came across the passage in Malachi 3. But this time I noticed a few verses that I had not seen before: " 'I will rebuke the devourer for your sakes [if you give of your tithes and offerings], so that he will not destroy the fruit of your ground, nor shall the vine fail to bear fruit for you in the field,' says the LORD of hosts." This is exactly what had happened to us! Because we were not contributing to the Church in any regular way, a "devourer" was swiping our income—gobbling it up! As a result, we were essentially destitute.

What I saw—or at least understood—for the first time was that the Lord promised to "open the windows of heaven and pour out a blessing" if only we would give freely to His work. He would "rebuke the devourer" if only we would make Him first in our pocketbook

as well as our hearts. That day Gail and I realized that we couldn't afford *not* to give regularly. Since our Church practiced tithing, consistency in giving was made much easier. From that moment on, the tithe has come first—before the bills, before a savings account, before groceries, before everything.

I wish I could say that our financial problems instantly disappeared. They didn't. Financial recovery was a slow and painful process. But at least we were back on track and had taken the first step toward financial (and spiritual!) responsibility.

At this point, I want to acknowledge that in many Orthodox circles contributions to the Church are made through pledges, special offerings, and other means. Almsgiving is always encouraged, as it has been throughout the centuries. If this is your situation, set up an appointment with your priest to determine how best you can serve God with your finances. Let him tell you what the needs of the Church are, and how you can best support them. Then, under his guidance, make up your mind to give sacrificially and wholeheartedly towards those needs.

GUIDELINES FOR TITHING

If you are going to tithe, or even if you have tithed for years, a few practical tips will come in handy. To save you a little time and pain, I've compiled a list of guidelines regarding tithing. Perhaps this list will be helpful.

1) **Pay the tithe first.** When you sit down to pay the bills, the first check you should write is a check to the Church. Don't look to see if you can afford it. You probably can't. Writing this check is an act of faith. Either Malachi 3:8-12 is true or it isn't.

2) **Figure the tithe on your gross income.** Take your total gross income and multiply by ten percent. Taxes are

an expense like any other expense. In the Old Testament, the tithe was to be paid on the first fruits of the harvest, before the deduction of expenses. Applying this truth to the modern situation, we should figure our tithe on the gross, not the net.

3) Pay the tithe to the Church. In the Old Covenant, the people were to pay their tithes to the Levitical priests, who represented the ecclesiastical order. In the New Covenant, the people brought their gifts to the Apostles (see Acts 5:1, 2). In a similar way, we pay our tithe to Christ by paying it to His Church.

4) Bring the tithe with you to the Divine Liturgy. Obviously, you could just drop your check in the mail and be done with it. In doing so, however, you miss the vital connection between tithing and worship. Tithing is the response we offer to God because of His rich bounty toward us. It is thus truly eucharistic in nature. When the connection between tithing and worship is lost, the practice quickly degenerates into a kind of deathly legalism, something that is stifling to true spirituality. Therefore, bring the tithe to Church and offer it to God as part of your heartfelt worship.

5) Don't give to other causes until you have first established a habit of faithful tithing. Tithing is a prerequisite to (or a beginning of) giving. All kinds of good causes—and some bad ones—come begging for support, but we should not consider giving to them until we have first become faithful in paying the tithe.

A FINAL CHALLENGE

In Malachi 3, God makes a statement that is made nowhere else in the Bible. He invites us to bring our finances into the storehouse and then "try" Him (Malachi 3:10). The word *try* in the Hebrew means to "test." To translate it into modern terms, the Lord is saying, "Give me a try. See if I will do what I say I will do. See if I won't open the heavens and pour out a blessing that is bigger than you can receive."

That is still God's challenge to us. He longs for us to test Him in this matter. He longs for the opportunity to prove to you that if you will put Him first, He will bless you beyond your wildest dreams.

Deacon Michael S. Hyatt
Nashville, Tennessee

From AGAIN Vol. 11, No. 3.
Original publication date: Fall, 1988

Questions for thought and discussion:

1) Discuss together the biblical basis of giving. What does it mean to you that:
a) everything belongs to God;
b) we are God's stewards;
c) we are held accountable for how we use the resources God gives us?

2) If God were to get the "leftovers" after all your bills were paid, how much do you think you would give during an average month? If you were to apply the "first fruits" principle, how much could you give?

3) Do you truly believe that God will "open the windows of heaven and pour out a blessing" when you give? Have you had personal experience of the "devourer" gobbling up your income?

THE BATTLE FOR THE BILLFOLD

Practical ideas that really work

BY FR. SIMEON BERVEN

A number-one aim in the lives of many people is to be "financially independent." This goal can literally dominate everything a person does with his time and money. It can so possess us, that a fantasy world develops and we lose touch with economic reality.

The statistics are overwhelmingly in favor of the average working person never attaining such financial independence. In a recent survey of Americans over sixty-five and retired, 88% were unsuccessfully retired. Imagine—the richest country in the world and nearly nine out of ten are short on funds after a lifetime of work.

There is an alternative way to find financial independence. British Bible translator J.B. Phillips did a masterful job on Romans 12:2: "Don't let the world pour you into its mold. . . ." Doesn't that happen more often than we care to admit with our money? Face it—we've become worldly. Whereas society calls for us to practice what I call the NBMM Syndrome (Newest, Best, Most expensive, Most popular), God promises to meet our needs, not our greeds!

FROM WANTS TO NEEDS

Perhaps the greatest change in my life regarding money came when my priorities changed from getting what I wanted, to getting what I needed. For the Scriptures do say, "My God shall supply all your *need* according to His riches in glory by Christ Jesus" (Philippians 4:19). This was the point at which I began to experience true financial security and independence.

In making the wants-to-needs switch, let me pass on to you some ideas that work. They come from business acquaintances, friends, consumer magazines, and personal trial and error. Any financial advisor will have his or her own list of suggestions, not always matching mine. However, the following are a few of the rules my wife and I have lived by and have found helpful over the years. These principles helped shake us loose from being consumer-oriented to becoming sharing-oriented. For the more we save, the more we can give to Christ, through His Church, to those in need.

GENERAL PRINCIPLES

1. Never buy new what you can buy used. The numbers here are amazing. Why buy a new car for $20,000 or more when you can buy a good used car for $8,000 or $5,000 or $3,500! With depreciation, the value of a new car drops about 25% when you drive it off the showroom floor. Consider, too, your savings when you buy good clean used

appliances, garden tools, and sports equipment.

2. Never make payments; always pay cash. Save until you can afford the purchase. The one exception to the rule is in the purchase of a home.

3. Don't charge more than you can pay off each month. Do plastic surgery on your wallet if necessary and remove your credit cards if they have control of you. Limit your credit cards to two, and shop around for low membership fees.

4. Buy only what you need or genuinely want. A bargain is never a bargain if the item is not useful in the first place.

5. Buy quality for lasting good service. Three pairs of quality shoes, for example, are always better than eight or ten pairs of cheap ones. Ditto for clothing, tools, and most other items.

SPECIFIC PURCHASES

With the general principles in place, let us turn to some major ticket purchases you'll make—some repeated—in your adult lifetime. Remember the goal: saving to give.

AUTOMOBILES

1. Many consumer advocates say the best auto bargain is a clean car two or three years old that you can drive into oblivion.

2. Want a relatively new car at significant savings? Consider a dealer demo or a rental agency car (Hertz, Avis, National) with 25,000 to 30,000 miles and a new car warranty. In 1967 we bought a Volkswagen Bug that had 4,000 dealer demo miles on it. We saved $800.00 on the sticker price, got the new car guarantee, and my wife still drives it almost daily [as of 1988]!

3. For bargain prices, a well-kept car of a non-spiffy model is ideal. Examples: a stick-shift Plymouth Valiant, Dodge Dart, or an AMC four-door sedan. The biggest savings are on clean cars nobody else wants.

4. My favorites: Older well-appointed, low-mileage, garage-kept General Motors top-of-the-line models. I still drive a used '69 Olds 98 convertible and love it! Occasional repairs are significantly cheaper than monthly payments.

5. Other hints: Check the glove compartment and the trunk. If these are clean to immaculate, odds are the rest of the car is too. Buy from private parties using cash, not a check—cash helps talk the price down. Ask a mechanic friend to check the car before you buy. A classic car will generally hold or increase its value. My convertible is worth much more today than when I purchased it.

APPLIANCES

1. Check a consumer magazine for brands with the best reputation for longevity. Generally, names like Zenith, GE, Maytag, Kenmore, and Gibson are best, but look for models not overloaded with repair-inducing "extras."

2. Shop estate sales. Items are sold to close out an estate, not because they are troublesome. Garage sales in good neighborhoods can produce bargains too, but be the early bird with cash in hand. Check the surroundings: a well-kept house and yard suggest carefully maintained items for sale.

3. Always ask why an item is on sale.

4. Take along a knowledgeable friend if possible.

5. Pay a bit more for something extra clean and smooth-working. Saving $25.00 on a ragged item needing "minor repair" is false economy.

GROCERIES

1. Supermarkets are best—and aim for one or two stops a week. Neighborhood convenience stores are more expensive.

2. Shop the sales—especially on meat—and stock up as your budget permits.

3. Shop after dinner! You'll be more objective.

4. Quantity saves. Giant-sized laundry soap, 10 pounds of potatoes, 20 pounds of charcoal, 18-pack eggs, and case lots of most things mean good savings.

6. Avoid come-ons. Something cheap that nobody wants to eat is too expensive.

7. Buy seasonally. Vegetables, fish, lamb, fruit, and pork have cheap and expensive seasons. We find excellent values on produce at our summertime "Farmer's Market."

"A bargain is never a bargain if the item is not useful in the first place."

PURCHASING A HOME

Besides the obvious advice—shop for a good loan, find a reputable realtor or attorney, make sure the place is termite inspected—here are some other value-oriented hints.

1. Map out the neighborhoods you want and can afford. Then, try to find the least expensive home in the best neighborhood—perhaps a home that needs some cosmetic work. These are usually the best values. In other words, a potentially nice home in a great neighborhood is a far better value than a great home in a poor neighborhood.

2. Choose a home that will have broad resale appeal. A bargain on an undesirable place will cost you dearly at resale time.

3. Look for potential. Would some shutters, a picket fence, a new paint job or trimmed hedge turn a Plain Jane into a showplace?

4. Experts say there are three criteria for home purchases: location, location, and location.

5. Watch for the nickel and dime traps. If a low-priced home needs major work—a new roof, plumbing, electrical and sewer repairs, paint, insulation, and concrete work—look elsewhere.

CLOTHING

1. Shop right after Christmas, Easter, and July 4th—the best times to buy clothing.

2. Go for brand-name, established store mark-downs—not slashed prices on budget items. Quality stores like Nordstrom, Saks, Daytons, Lord and Taylor, and Hudson Bay feature good sales and bargains. Watch for sales at Sears or other large department stores, as they discount items heavily at certain times of the year.

3. Find factory outlet places with top brands.

4. Plan your wardrobe needs in advance. Bargains on suits, shoes and shirts, dresses, and blouses are no savings at all unless you need them.

5. Leading mail-order catalogs like Lands End and L L. Bean feature good staple items, and stand by their products with full refunds.

FURNITURE AND HOUSEHOLD ITEMS

1. Generally, the advice for appliances holds true with furniture: look for name brands at estate sales or at yard and garage sales in established neighborhoods.

2. Fair-priced antiques have at least three advantages: (a) they should hold or increase their value; (b) a few nicks and scratches from your children might even add "character"; (c) good antique furniture is often better built

and more durable than new furniture.

3. Buy traditional pieces when possible—avoid "fad" items.

4. When you set up housekeeping consider buying good *used* sheets, towels, silverware, dishes, utensils, brooms, pots and pans. Savings are usually substantial.

INVESTING

Providing for the future now means freedom to be good stewards in the years ahead. There are a number of investment opportunities to choose from.

1. Real Estate. Home ownership is an outstanding investment almost everywhere, especially on the West Coast and the Northeast. A few rental units can be wise—if you can handle the (a) upkeep, (b) record keeping, and (c) dealing with sometimes problematic tenants.

2. Mutual Funds. When you locate good ones, you can usually invest with little or no checking up. Watch for no-load or low-load funds with dependable track records in places like *Money Magazine* and diversify among a few safe ones. But remember, the market moves up and down. A long-term stable return is better than a high-risk short-term.

3. Certificate of Deposit or Money Market Funds. These have served me best. If possible, lock into an established *high* rate of interest. They are great for people with no time or desire to devote to their finances, or those with delicate stomachs and insomnia!

4. IRAs. In my opinion, still a bargain for the middle-class investor.

5. When the children are grown and gone, and you have a good equity in your home, consider selling and renting. There is a good tax break if you're over fifty-five. We sold our home in Seattle in 1979 and have lived comfortably renting. The income I receive from investing the proceeds more than covers rental payments.

BANKING

In recent years, banking has gotten costly. Here are some money-saving tips:

1. Avoid annual-fee credit cards. Once your credit is established, watch for offers from reputable no-fee and low-fee cards.

2. Saving accounts: Watch for no-minimum-balance accounts at regular interest rates. Often new banks or branches offer the best fee scales.

> ## "You and I are caretakers of what we have been given. We can either mismanage it or be faithful to our charge from God."

---

3. Checking accounts: a no-minimum-deposit, no-fee, unlimited-check, interest-bearing program is what you want. They are tough to find, but ask around.

4. If you are a student, or a senior citizen like me, ask about free banking services. And watch your statement! Although I had qualified for no-fee service, through a computer error I was charged $7.50 a month for regular services.

A FINANCIAL GAME PLAN

There are four very important things to keep in mind. Firstly, have a good cash savings plan. Secondly, keep adequate insurance coverage. Thirdly, develop a satisfactory investment program. Fourthly, be sure to have a will.

Having a good cash account has given me leverage to buy the things that I need, and to give tithes and offerings to the Church. Having a good insurance program has brought me through auto and health emergencies, and I have the assurance that my family will be covered when I depart. Through the investment plan I have a lifelong income without being a drain on other people. And in my will there is direction for disbursement that will be helpful to both family and God's Kingdom.

We as God's people are called to be good stewards of all that we possess. You and I are caretakers of what we have been given. We can either mismanage it or be faithful to our charge from God.

Everything we have belongs to God. When we do our part, He, as usual, overdoes His part. Take His challenge and let Him prove what He has promised for your life!

Fr. Simeon Berven
Ss. Peter & Paul Orthodox Church
Ben Lomond, California

From AGAIN Vol. 11, No. 3
Original publication date: September, 1988

Questions for thought and discussion:

1) Think honestly about your own attitudes towards money. How important is financial independence to you? Is it your priority to get what you want, or to get what you need? Would you characterize yourself as a consumer-oriented person or a sharing-oriented person?

2) Discuss the principle "never buy new what you can buy used." What items are you comfortable buying used? To what extent are you influenced by the "newest, best, most expensive" syndrome?

3) Discuss the principles "never make payments; always pay cash" and "don't charge more than you can pay off each month." To what extent have you used credit cards in the past? Do they have control over you?

4) Discuss the principle "buy quality for lasting good service." When you are making a purchase, how do price and quality enter into your decision-making process?

5) Think about your investment goals. What types of investments have you already made, and what types of investments would you like to consider in the future? Are you looking for investments with a high rate of return, or with steady growth and low risk?

6) Map out a financial game plan for your married life. What are your goals, hopes, and expectations during the following phases of your life:
   a) your early-married, child-raising years;
   b) your mid-life, peak-career years;
   c) your retirement years and old age?

7) Whom do you depend upon for financial advice? If you were to run into financial difficulties, to whom would you turn?

SPENDING WISELY

HELPFUL HINTS ON HOUSEHOLD BUDGETING
BY FR. TROY MASHBURN

"BILLS, BILLS, BILLS!"

Budget? Who, me? Why should I take the time to read an article about setting up a tedious, time-consuming family budget?

Besides, I thought AGAIN Magazine was devoted to calling Christians back to their roots in historic Christianity. What do worldly topics like income and expenditures have to do with a spiritually oriented periodical?

The answer to all the above questions can be found in one simple yet profoundly spiritual word: *stewardship.* True Christians are called to be stewards of *all* things—both spiritual and material—within their possession. This definitely includes money, and more particularly the way we spend it. It is our responsibility to manage our finances wisely and to keep track of what God in His goodness has allotted to us.

A simple household budget can make that task much less painful, and much more effective. And such a budget can enable us to give even when we think it is impossible!

A properly prepared, maintained, and monitored budget will allow us to: 1) tithe from our income; 2) meet normal fiscal responsibilities; 3) deal with unexpected events; and 4) contribute beyond the tithe to other needs.

THE STARTING PLACE

Many, if not most, people are intimidated by trying to keep a budget. Such concern is unwarranted. Keeping a budget is no more difficult than keeping a checkbook. However, as with a checkbook, daily attention is a necessity.

There are two requirements to begin keeping a family budget.

1) Personal commitment. The most important aspect of accomplishing any task is to commit your time and effort to the endeavor. This is especially true in initiating and keeping a household budget. You must set your heart, mind, and will to begin and to maintain your budget daily.

2) A record-keeping book. Having made the commitment, you must purchase a budget record book. Office supply stores usually have several types. The best ones list income and the total paid out for each day. The daily total paid out is further broken down by type of expenditure. I have included a very simple example at the end of this article. There are also a number of good personal computer software programs available. However, unless you are already a proficient and regular computer user, I suggest starting with a manual system.

BUDGET SETTING

With those two requirements in hand, you can begin the process of setting up and maintaining your actual budget. The first step is to plan out your income and expenses.

Income is generally easy to estimate. Figure in your after-tax wage and salary income for the period you will receive it. My only caution is to avoid overestimating your income from sources other than a fixed monthly salary (i.e. commissions, bonuses, interest and dividends from investments).

The more difficult area is to plan expenditures, and these should be planned for the next twelve months. I suggest the following order of priority in estimating your spending:

1) The Kingdom—A consistent portion of your income should be allocated to the Kingdom of God. If you tithe, it should be taken out on the front end of your paycheck, not as a tack-on after all the other expenses have been met under the guise, "I'll wait and see if there is that much left."

2) Necessities—Food, shelter, a reasonable clothing allowance, etc. Remember that some items are paid quarterly, some semi-annually, and some annually. Pest control and auto insurance are examples of periodic non-monthly payments.

3) Savings—Work toward a total savings amount equal to three to six months of your income. Unless you make savings a priority, it will never happen!

4) Other items. This order assumes that you have adequate medical, life, and disability insurance premiums withheld from your paycheck. If you are self-employed, these items should then be included as necessities.

TRAPS TO AVOID

There are also a number of snares to avoid. They are too numerous to enumerate, but in passing, let me mention several notorious traps to watch out for.

• "I want it, therefore I must need it." Not so. Check yourself carefully here before signing on the dotted line. For example, a brand new VCR with portable mini-cam might be nice to own, but it's definitely not in the same category as groceries and rent. You must honestly evaluate what is necessary and what is not.

• "I can't afford it, but I *can* borrow." Don't be caught by this trap. Spend within your means—put off that discretionary purchase until you have the money.

• "My brain says 'no' but my heart says 'now.' " Never allow your passion for possessions to overcome your God-given reason.

• "I can always put this on my credit card." Be careful, it's addictive. The best rule of thumb is, "When in doubt, don't."

• "If I stretch my income, I can just make those payments." Just because your income equals your expenses you are not necessarily out of the woods. There should always be some measure of flex to allow for the unexpected.

• Lastly, be sure as you are setting up your budget to set realistic goals for yourself and your family. Too many people set out to undo in one or two months habits which have taken years to develop. When failure sets in, they give up in frustration. Be sure those new goals are realistic and achievable.

HOUSEHOLD BUDGET

MONTH OF *June*, 19 *96*

Date	Description	Income	Total Paid	Tithe / Charity	Savings	Groceries	Eating Out	Rent	Utilities	Repairs	Furniture	Clothing	Gas	Auto Repair	Medical	Entertainment	Other
						Food		Housing					Auto				
	BUDGET	2400	2400	240	100	600	40	500	100	20	50	100	100	50	50	75	375
5/1	ABC rental		500					500									
5/4	Safeway		150			150											
5/4	Porch lamp		35								35						
5/6	Cash Check		30													20	10
5/8	Penney's		70									70					
5/10	Plumber		50							50							
5/11	Exxon		65										65				
5/15	A & P Market		120			120											
5/15	Paycheck	1200															
5/15	St Geroge's		120	120													
5/15	First Federal Bank		50		50												
5/15	Termite Control		100														100
5/16	AT & T		35						35								
	SUBTOTALS	1200	1325	120	50	370		500	35	50	35	70	65			20	110

The above sample "Household Budget" page gives one example of a simple method for tracking your spending on a monthly basis. On the back of this page is a blank form that you can photocopy and modify to suit your own needs. There are also many computer programs on the market that not only help track a family budget, but also balance your checkbook, record items for income tax purposes, and provide other financial helps.

HOUSEHOLD BUDGET: MONTH OF _____, 19 __

SUBTOTALS				BUDGET	Date
					Description
					Income
					Total Paid
					Tithe / Charity
					Savings
					Groceries — Food
					Eating Out — Food
					Rent — Housing
					Utilities — Housing
					Repairs — Housing
					Furniture — Housing
					Clothing
					Gas — Auto
					Auto Repair — Auto
					Medical
					Entertainment
					Other

RECORD KEEPING

The most important aspect of record keeping is to do it daily. Just as we observe liturgical hours of prayer for our spiritual well-being and self-control, we ought to observe (pardon me) "liturgical record keeping." Forget about trying to remember what you spent last week—you can't. Do it today—every day!

Accurately keeping track of how you spend your cash is very difficult and therefore the source of much "frittered" money.

I suggest the following pointers to help keep up.

1) Write checks for cash as seldom as possible. Use checks whenever possible to pay your bills. A debit card can also be used.

2) Cash the same size check every time. I suggest an amount no larger than what you will spend "out of pocket" in one week.

3) Keep a wallet or pocket pad record of how you spend your cash.

4) When you cash your next check, use your spending record to write down the expenditures. Note the cashed check in the example on page 209.

One area which should be mentioned here is the area of credit cards. They greatly complicate a simple system. For that reason, as well as others, I suggest—in order of my preference—the following alternatives to approaching the use of cards: 1) Don't use them. 2) Use a debit card. It's just like writing a check. Be sure to keep the debit slips, since you will need to use them to do your record keeping. 3) If you must use plastic, pay off your credit card bill monthly and do so the same day each month. Post your records from the charge tickets paid on the bill paid.

> # "When in doubt, don't."

REVIEW

The last step in developing a budget is by far the most important—the review. I recommend that this be done at least once a week. Subtotal your expenses and compare with your planned expenditures. How are you doing relative to budget? Have you made or lost ground? What adjustments do you need to make in your plans? Can you make any of those desired purchases you didn't budget, or will you have to cut back on your plans?

By the way, budgets have gotten too much bad press in our day and age. Far from being a masochistic instrument of self-denial and deprivation, a properly tuned budget can actually free you up to purchase things—without guilt—you could never in good conscience have purchased before.

At the end of the month, you should summarize the month's activity and show how much over or under you were on each category. Also compare these totals with your checkbook to make sure they agree. The example on page 209 will give you an idea of how your budget should look. It is not intended to be complete. Certainly more categories are needed, and to save space, only part of a month has been included. (A blank copy of this form which you can use as a master to photocopy your own budget sheets is given on page 210.)

These are the basics of keeping a personal budget—how to get started. I believe that if you diligently pursue a personal budgeting regimen, you will find yourself managing your financial affairs rather than being managed by them.

Furthermore, you will be able to contribute to the Kingdom of God and better oversee the possessions with which God has entrusted you.

May the Holy Spirit help us all to be faithful in our God-given responsibilities.

Fr. Troy Mashburn practiced as a CPA for seven years before serving as chief financial officer for a privately owned manufacturing company in the mid-South. He is also a priest at St. John's Orthodox Church in Memphis, Tennessee.

From AGAIN Vol. 11, No. 3
Original publication date: September, 1988

Questions for thought and discussion:

1) What is your first reaction to the subject of budgeting? Do you tend to believe that maintaining a household budget is a tedious chore? Or do you tend to believe that maintaining a household budget is an important and appropriate way to responsibly manage your finances and to "keep track of what God in His goodness has allotted to us"?

2) Evaluate yourself honestly. How often do you fall into the traps of thinking:
    a) "I want it, therefore I must need it";
    b) "I can't afford it, but I can borrow";
    c) "my brain says 'no' but my heart says 'now' "?
If falling into these "traps" is a common occurrence for you, how can you begin to establish new patterns for your financial decision-making?

3) How often has decision-making regarding how to spend money caused friction in your relationship? What has been the most common financial problem in your relationship? Do you think establishing and living by a budget could help you prevent this type of conflict in the future? If so, are you both willing to commit yourselves to implementing a budget?

List of References

Documents of the Orthodox Church in America: Marriage, Syosett, NY: Encyclical Letter of the Holy Synod of Bishops of the Orthodox Church in America

Elisabeth Behr-Sigel, *The Place of the Heart,* Torrance, CA: Oakwood Publications, 1992

Anthony Coniaris, *Getting Ready for Marriage in the Orthodox Church,* Minneapolis, MN: Light and Life Press, 1982

Elchaninov, *Diary of a Russian Priest,* Crestwood, NY: St. Vladimir's Seminary Press, 1982

Fr. Paul Evdokimov, *The Sacrament of Love,* Crestwood, NY: St. Vladimir's Seminary Press, 1985

George Gabriel, *You Call My Words Immodest,* British Columbia, Canada: Synaxis Press, 1994

Stanley Harakas, *Guidelines for Marriage in the Orthodox Church,* Minneapolis, MN: Light and Life Press, 1970

Dr. Peter Kallelis, *Holy Matrimony: Marriage in the Orthodox Church*, Westfield, NJ: Ecumenical Publications, 1984

Vladimir Lossky, *Orthodox Theology: An Introduction,* Crestwood, NY: St. Vladimir's Seminary Press, 1989

Wayne Mack, *Preparing for Marriage,* Tulsa, Oklahoma: Virgil Hensley Publishing, 1986

Margaret Mead, *Male and Female,* New York, NY: William Morrow and Company, 1967

Fr. John Meyendorff, *Marriage: An Orthodox Perspective,* Crestwood, NY: St. Vladimir's Seminary Press, 1984

Monk Moses, *Married Saints of the Church,* Wildwood, CA: St. Xenia Skete, 1991

Philip Schaff and Henry Wace, editors, *Nicene and Post-Nicene Fathers,* Grand Rapids, MI: Wm. B. Eerdmans Publishing Company, (different publication dates for different volumes in the series)

Bishop Alexander (Semenoff-Tian-Chansky), *Life of Fr. John of Kronstadt,* Crestwood, NY: St. Vladimir's Seminary Press, 1979

Judson Swihart, *How Do You Say I Love You?,* Downers Grove, IL: InterVarsity Press, 1977

Paul Tournier, *To Understand Each Other,* Louisville, KY: Westminster John Knox, 1966

Benedicta Ward, *The Sayings of the Desert Fathers,* Kalamazoo, MI:

Cistercian Publications, 1975

Bishop Kallistos (Ware), *The Orthodox Way,* Crestwood, NY: St. Vladimir's Seminary Press, 1990